Suzan D. McGinnis
Editor

P9-AOP-619

Electronic Collection Management

Electronic Collection Management has been co-published simultaneously as *Collection Management,* Volume 25, Number 1/2 2000.

Pre-publication
REVIEWS,
COMMENTARIES,
EVALUATIONS . . .

"**E**ditor Suzan McGinnis's introduction emphasizes the need for collection development principles to remain pertinent yet flexible in this era of periodicals aggregators, consortial buying, and e-books. Strong collections, be they print or in some other format, require thoughtful construction. This timely volume considers ways to maintain that level of thought even into the future."

Diane J. Graves, MLN, Dean
Library and Information Services
Hollins University
Roanoke, VA

More pre-publication
REVIEWS, COMMENTARIES, EVALUATIONS . . .

"*E*lectronic Collection Management is clearly a reflection of its time. It mirrors a situation which is new enough that practitioners are balancing the values of and needs for traditional collections which overlap with the swift, complex, and expensive demands of electronic collections. It also reflects circumstances that have progressed enough so that even small academic libraries are caught up in issues similar to those of libraries with budgets many times larger.

McGinnis's book will be of particular use to libraries that are beginning to see a greater demand for electronic resources beyond basic indexing and abstracting services. In particular, Newman's article carefully spells out a series of decision points for the implementation of electronic resources; Oliver's informative article on SPARC indicates scholarly communication publishing alternatives to the increasingly expensive commercial ones; and Peters' interpretation of current research will generate fruitful discussion of the future of collection development and management."

Joan B. Fiscella, PhD, AMLS
Associate Professor
University of Illinois at Chicago
Library

"*E*lectronic Collection Management covers the broad array of issues that face collection managers as we face transition to electronic publications. Suzan McGinnis has assembled an excellent team of writers who cover the past, present and future concerns of electronic collection management

We are running two kinds of libraries right now, the print and the electronic. The tensions we face as a result of this are addressed here in a pragmatic and thought-provoking manner. Information about initiatives such as SPARC, the developing field of interdisciplinary studies that are supported by this new technology, and new ways of organizing and accessing electronic resources are covered here by practitioners who are immersed in these issues on a daily basis.

The volume is readable and well-documented and a clear reflection of the issues we face today and in the future."

Karen Schmidt, PhD
Associate University Librarian
for Collections
University of Illinois
at Urbana-Champaign

Electronic Collection Management

Electronic Collection Management has been co-published simultaneously as *Collection Management*, Volume 25, Numbers 1/2 2000.

The *Collection Management* Monographic "Separates"

Below is a list of "separates," which in serials librarianship means a special issue simultaneously published as a special journal issue or double-issue *and* as a "separate" hardbound monograph. (This is a format which we also call a "Docuserial.")

"Separates" are published because specialized libraries or professionals may wish to purchase a specific thematic issue by itself in a format which can be separately cataloged and shelved, as opposed to purchasing the journal on an on-going basis. Faculty members may also more easily consider a "separate" for classroom adoption.

"Separates" are carefully classified separately with the major book jobbers so that the journal tie-in can be noted on new book order slips to avoid duplicate purchasing.

You may wish to visit the Haworth's website at . . .

http://www.HaworthPress.com

. . . to search our online catalog for complete tables of contents of these separates and related publications.

You may also call 1-800-HAWORTH (outside US/Canada: 607-722-5857), or Fax 1-800-895-0582 (outside US/Canada: 607-771-0012), or e-mail at:

getinfo@haworthpressinc.com

Electronic Collection Management, edited by Suzan D. McGinnis (Vol. 25, No. 1/2, 2000) *A practical guide to the art and science of acquiring and organizing electronic resources.*

Creating New Strategies for Cooperative Collection Development, edited by Milton T. Wolf and Marjorie E. Bloss (Vol. 24, No. (1/2)(3/4), 2000) *Discusses current initiatives in cooperative collection development and points the way to expanding the scope of this activity in the future.*

Cooperative Collection Development: Significant Trends and Issues, edited by Donald B. Simpson (Vol. 23, No. 4, 1998) *Shows how the art of cooperation requires librarians' ability to comprehend and support "big picture" goals and the skills to incorporate "common good" objectives into local activities so that there is constructive and affirmative benefit to your own programs and services.*

Government Information Collections in the Networked Environment: New Issues and Models, edited by Joan F. Cheverie (Vol. 23, No. 3, 1998) *Explores the challenging issues related to effective access to government information.*

Going Digital: Strategies for Access, Preservation, and Conversion of Collections to a Digital Format, edited by Donald L DeWitt (Vol. 22, No. 3/4, 1998) *"This excellent book presents a comprehensive study of crucial issues confronting librarians and archivists today. . . . From the first article to the last, it is a compelling read!" (Carol A. Mathius, MLIS, CA, Archivist, Head of Special Collections, Nicholls State University, Thibodaux, Louisiana)*

Collection Development: Access in the Virtual Library, edited by Maureen Pastine (Vol. 22, No. 1/2, 1997) *"Documents unequivocably that collaboration–between library and customer, library and vendor, and among libraries–is essential for success in today's academic library." (Kathryn Hammell carpenter, MS, University Librarian, Valparaiso University, Indiana)*

Collection Development: Past and Future, edited by Maureen Pastine (Vol. 21, No. 2/3, 1996) *"An important navigational tool for steering through the turbulent waters of the evolving collection development environment. I highly recommend it." (Blake Landar, PhD, Philosophy, Classics, and Religion Bibliographer, University of Florida)*

Electronic Resources: Implications for Collection Management, edited by Genevieve S. Ownes (Vol. 21, No. 1, 1996) *"Discusses the strengths and weaknesses of electronic resources, as well as the implications these resources have on collection management. Also provides guidance on incorporating electronic resources into library collections." (Reference and Research Book News)*

Practical Issues in Collection Development and Collection Access, edited by Katina Strauch, Sally W. Somers, Susan Zappen, and Anne Jennings (Vol. 19, No. 3/4, 1995) *With surveys, studies, and first-hand accounts of "how we did it," this book shows how fellow professionals view the evolving world of information selection, maintenance, access, and delivery.*

Access Services in Libraries: New Solutions for Collection Management, edited by Gregg Sapp (Vol. 17, No. 1/2, 1993) *"Develops a theoretical foundation for the growing phenomenon of access services in public and academic libraries–an approach to the increasingly complex problem of making materials available to patrons." (Reference and Research Book News)*

Euro-Librarianship: Shared Resources, Shared Responsibilities, edited by Assunta Pisani, (Vol. 15, No. 1/2/3/4, 1992) *"A rich compendium of information about European studies, especially in relation to librarianship. . . . A worthwhile volume that will be helpful to Western European Studies librarians for many years to come." (Western European Specialists Section Newsletter)*

International Conference on Research Library Cooperation, The Research Libraries Group, Inc. (Vol. 9, No. 2/3, 1998) *"A useful . . . look at selected cooperative schemes in Britain, Europe and the United States and propose guidelines for the future." (Library Association Record)*

Reading and the Art of Librarianship: Selected Essays of John B. Nicholson, Jr. edited by Paul Z. DuBois and Dean H. Keller (Vol. 8, No. 3/4, 1986) *"A selection from over 300 completely delightful essays, representing the late author's wide and varied interests. There is much food for thought in these pages, a lively collection that is personal, intimate . . . a passionate look at the world of books." (Academic Library Book Review)*

Collection Management for School Library Media Centers, edited by Brenda H. White (Vol. 7, No. 3/4, 1986) *"A wealth of information concerning managing a school library media center collection. . . . Readable, interesting, and practical." (The Book Report: The Journal for Junior and Senior High School Librarians)*

The State of Western European Studies: Implication for Collection Development, edited by Anthony M. Angiletta, Martha L. Brogan, Charles S. Fineman, and Clara M. Lovett (Vol. 6, No. 1/2, 1984) *"An exceptionally well-edited volume . . . lively and engrossing. . . . An informative and thought-provoking overview of the current state of Western European studies and its possible future directions." (Special Libraries Association)*

Published by

The Haworth Information Press, 10 Alice Street, Binghamton, NY 13904-1580 USA

The Haworth Information Press is an imprint of the Haworth Press, Inc., 10 Alice Street, Binghamton, NY 13904-1580 USA.

Electronic Collection Management has been co-published simultaneously as *Collection Management,* Volume 25, Numbers 1/2 2000.

Cover design by Thomas J. Mayshock Jr.

Library of Congress Cataloging-in-Publication Data

Electronic collection managment / Suzan D. McGinnis, editor.
        p. cm.
        "Co-published simultaneously as Collection management, v. 25, nos. 1/2 2000."
        Includes bibliographical references and index.
        ISBN 0-7890-1308-8 (alk. paper)–ISBN 0-7890-1309-6 (pbk. : alk. paper)
        1. Libraries–United States–Special collections–Electronic information resources. 2. Academic libraries–Collection development–United States. 3. Electronic information resources–United States.
I. McGinnis, Suzan D. II. Collection management.
Z692.C65 E42 2000
025.2′84–dc21   00-053864

Electronic Collection Management

Suzan D. McGinnis
Editor

Electronic Collection Management has been co-published simultaneously as *Collection Management,* Volume 25, Numbers 1/2 2000.

The Haworth Information Press
An imprint of
The Haworth Press, Inc.
New York • London • Oxford

Indexing, Abstracting & Website/Internet Coverage

This section provides you with a list of major indexing & abstracting services. That is to say, each service began covering this periodical during the year noted in the right column. Most Websites which are listed below have indicated that they will either post, disseminate, compile, archive, cite or alert their own Website users with research-based content from this work. (This list is as current as the copyright date of this publication.)

Abstracting, Website/Indexing Coverage ...... Year When Coverage Began

- *BUBL Information Service, an Internet-based Information Service for the UK higher education community <URL: http://bubl.ac.uk/>* **1995**

- *Central Library & Documentation Bureau* **1995**

- *CNPIEC Reference Guide: Chinese National Directory of Foreign Periodicals* **1995**

- *Combined Health Information Database (CHID)* **1995**

- *Current Awareness Abstracts* **1991**

- *Current Cities (& Websites)* **2000**

- *FINDEX <www.publist.com>* **1999**

- *FRANCIS INIST/CNRS* **1983**

- *IBZ International Bibliography of Periodical Literature* **1995**

- *Index to Periodical Articles Related to Law* **1989**

- *Information Reports & Bibliographies* **1992**

- *Information Science Abstracts* **1989**

(continued)

Book reviews are selectively excerpted by the Guide to Professional Literature of the Journal of Academic Librarianship.

Special Bibliographic Notes related to special journal issues (separates) and indexing/abstracting:

- indexing/abstracting services in this list will also cover material in any "separate" that is co-published simultaneously with Haworth's special thematic journal issue or DocuSerial. Indexing/abstracting usually covers material at the article/chapter level.
- monographic co-editions are intended for either non-subscribers or libraries which intend to purchase a second copy for their circulating collections.
- monographic co-editions are reported to all jobbers/wholesalers/approval plans. The source journal is listed as the "series" to assist the prevention of duplicate purchasing in the same manner utilized for books-in-series.
- to facilitate user/access services all indexing/abstracting services are encouraged to utilize the co-indexing entry note indicated at the bottom of the first page of each article/chapter/contribution.
- this is intended to assist a library user of any reference tool (whether print, electronic, online, or CD-ROM) to locate the monographic version if the library has purchased this version but not a subscription to the source journal.
- individual articles/chapters in any Haworth publication are also available through the Haworth Document Delivery Service (HDDS).

ABOUT THE EDITOR

Suzan D. McGinnis holds the M.L.I.S degree from the University of Wisconsin-Milwaukee. Most of her professional library career has been in collection management, beginning with her first position as Collection Development Librarian at Augustana College in Rock Island, Illinois. She is currently Assistant Head of Information Service for Liaison and Collection Development at Texas Tech University Libraries, Lubbock, Texas. She has published articles in *Collection Management* and *Library Acquisitions Practice and Theory*, and she has presented several papers at library professional meetings.

Electronic Collection Management

CONTENTS

Preface

This volume seeks to focus on the variety of approaches and beliefs held by librarians across the country when it comes to electronic collection management. It has long been my belief that collection development is a cross between an art and a science. We look towards use counts and holdings in other libraries, but we also trust our collection librarians to be able to develop a sense of their collections and those of our neighbors across the world.

This art and science of collection building carries over into the electronic arena. This volume identifies some of the more talked about topics in electronic collection management, from the view of the small college library to the large research library. The collecting, evaluating, organizing, seeking of alternatives and leveraging of collections are all addressed, along with a look to the future.

Suzan D. McGinnis

[Haworth co-indexing entry note]: "Preface." McGinnis, Suzan D. Co-published simultaneously in *Collection Management* (The Haworth Information Press, an imprint of The Haworth Press, Inc.) Vol. 25, No. 1/2, 2000, p. xi; and: *Electronic Collection Management* (ed: Suzan D. McGinnis) The Haworth Information Press, an imprint of The Haworth Press, Inc., 2000, p. xi. Single or multiple copies of this article are available for a fee from The Haworth Document Delivery Service [1-800-342-9678, 9:00 a.m. - 5:00 p.m. (EST). E-mail address: getinfo@haworthpressinc.com].

Cultivating Our Garden:
The Impact of Digital Full Text Periodicals
on the Liberal Arts College Library

Barbara Doyle-Wilch
Carla Tracy

Although the 18-21-year-old undergraduate student's research strategy always has been governed by the "law of least effort," the availability of electronic full text journals has intensified the consequences of this approach. For the small liberal arts college, whose mission is founded upon a dedication to individualized, high quality undergraduate education, this has resulted in increased tensions concerning their highly focused collections; the librarians' ability to play an integral role in the educational process; and relationships with faculty. In addition, the tuition-driven nature of the liberal arts college's existence may cause the library to spend more time and money on being fully "wired" than on focusing the collection on the students' educational needs. This article examines these tensions and looks briefly at what the future may hold.

Let us begin with a fable:

> *Imagine that you are a descendant of Candide, blissfully cultivating your garden. To grow your vegetables, you need seeds, a hoe, water and sunshine. You have all of these in sufficient measure, as well as plenty of local buyers who are eager to buy "Candide's Cucumbers," your specialty.*

[Haworth co-indexing entry note]: "Cultivating Our Garden: The Impact of Digital Full Text Periodicals on the Liberal Arts College Library." Doyle-Wilch, Barbara, and Carla Tracy. Co-published simultaneously in *Collection Management* (The Haworth Information Press, an imprint of The Haworth Press, Inc.) Vol. 25, No. 1/2, 2000, pp. 1-16; and: *Electronic Collection Management* (ed: Suzan D. McGinnis) The Haworth Information Press, an imprint of The Haworth Press, Inc., 2000, pp. 1-16. Single or multiple copies of this article are available for a fee from The Haworth Document Delivery Service [1-800-342-9678, 9:00 a.m. - 5:00 p.m. (EST). E-mail address: getinfo@haworthpressinc.com].

Then one day, seeds for the new "super veggie" hybrid are ready for purchase. The super veggie is deliciously sweet and fast growing. Everyone wants it. However, the seeds are expensive and special conditions are needed. New tools and fertilizer are a must. Most problematic is the other hybrid–the "pseudo veggie"–that must be interspersed with the super veggie in order to control insects and other predators. These plants look just like the super veggie, grow even faster, and sometimes taste better, especially to young adults. It is impossible to efficiently harvest the super veggies without including the pseudos as well. The consumer must take the time to carefully examine each vegetable because, if eaten in large quantities, the pseudo veggies will cause illness.

Meanwhile, many of your buyers have moved away and those remaining will go to any garden where the super veggies are most readily available. In their enthusiasm for the wonderful new food, they do not recognize the difference between the super and pseudo veggies and certainly do not understand the dangers. In a way, you would like to go back to raising only Candide's Cucumbers. These are your heritage, and they are still in demand, especially by your older patrons. But if you don't offer super veggies, you will seriously endanger your business. And, after all, the super veggies are very tasty and nutritious when used appropriately.

So you run around your garden spending more money, buying more land, using more tools and fertilizers, and trying to find ways to caution buyers about the possible dangers. Very few of your buyers listen carefully, and the young buyers are by nature risk-takers who are even harder to convince. And if you make the process too difficult, they will just go to a different garden to get what they want. Soon you are spending most of your time, energy, and funds on the super veggies, and Candide's Cucumbers often are forgotten. In your few quiet moments, when you survey your garden from your house on the hill, you feel that it is hardly recognizable. You long for the day when things will settle down, when you can feel in control again . . .

Although libraries have changed dramatically over the past twenty years, the undergraduate student's desire to get the required number of resources–any resources–in the least possible amount of time is not new. Scott Van Dam and Scott R. DiMarco observed that undergraduates usually have a time management strategy, not a research strategy.[1] Or perhaps even closer to the truth is that the proverbial "law of least effort" is not just the law of undergraduate nature, but the law of human nature. Presented with the need to find information, all of us are likely first to try the approach that will strike the best balance between quality information and the speed of obtaining it. The crucial point, of course, is any individual's ability to judge "quality information" given the purpose of the research. By definition, the undergraduate is in the early stages of learning how to judge which sources of information are appropriate for the task at hand, and therefore most likely to allow–quite possibly without even realizing it–efficiency and speed to become all-important.

Until the mid-1980s, undergraduates probably began their research by going to the *Reader's Guide to Periodical Literature* or to another print index to find the periodical resources required for their assignments. Indexes to scholarly journals were separate from indexes to "popular" materials, and both were equally easy or difficult to use (except, perhaps, the dreaded abstracting services!). Students went to the stacks to find journals owned by their library. They read articles, took notes, and left the library as soon as possible. "ASAP" was measured in day*s*.

The advent of photocopiers and efficient interlibrary loan began the significant change in this long-standing routine. Periodicals could be located on the shelves, articles copied and carried from the library to be used at the student's convenience. If the library did not own a much-needed resource, interlibrary loan could provide a copy, often delivered directly to the student's mailbox. Long days spent in the library with pencils and note cards were no longer a staple of the undergraduate's life.

The appearance of electronic periodical indexes in the mid-1980s significantly increased the speed of research. Now subjects could be combined for a much more rapid and precise search. Keyword searching opened an entirely new way of accessing pertinent articles. The addition of abstracts to periodical indexes increased the ease of finding information. And then, just a few years ago, the explosive change occurred: digital full text articles. Now, any article that is instantly available in electronic full text–regardless of its appropriateness–is nearly irresistible to the busy undergraduate. It can be found quickly, printed immediately (perhaps free-of-charge or on one's own printer), and taken from the library. "ASAP" now is measured in *minutes.* In comparison to digital full text periodicals, the attractiveness of a library's paper journals–buried in the stacks; checked out or missing; costly and time-consuming to copy–has declined dramatically.

The transition to digitized resources in libraries has been widely discussed at nearly every professional conference and meeting and in the literature for the past decade. Many different titles have been used in the literature–such as "Nailing Jell-O to the Wall,"[2] "What Will Collection Developers Do?"[3] "Virtual Dreams Give Way to Digital Reality"[4] and "Beyond Access: New Concepts, New Tensions for Collection Development in a Digital Environment"[5]–to describe the tensions that this transition is causing in libraries. Also, over the past ten years, we have seen new job titles appear as libraries strive to manage the new formats: Digital Resources Librarian, Scholarly Communications Librarian, Electronic Resources Librarian, etc. While libraries of all sizes and missions are experiencing the tensions brought about by the rapid increase in digital resources, the feelings are exacerbated in small liberal arts colleges, where missions, financial resources and staffing have remained relatively unchanged.

At Augustana College, the entire library staff is composed of twenty people, including eight MLS librarians. Each librarian selects materials, works as liaison with an academic division, provides library instruction and works at the reference desk. There are only 150 full-time faculty and a long history of a core curriculum. Librarians and faculty at Augustana (and at many other colleges like it) have carefully developed highly focused collections that support the curriculum and the research needs of the students. A change that might be experienced as a ripple at a large university is highly intense and personal at a small college. The mass infusion of electronic serials has created tensions between librarians and faculty, between vendors and librarians, between students and faculty, and between libraries. The management of the library's relatively small budget is stressed by the overlap of print and electronic formats. In addition, the tuition-driven nature of the liberal arts college's existence may tempt the library to spend more time and money on being fully "wired" in an effort to maintain college enrollment than on focusing their resources for their students' educational needs. This article examines these new and increased tensions and their impact on the liberal arts college library.

TENSIONS

Tension #1: Quality Control

Like many other liberal arts colleges, Augustana College has developed its print collections for over one hundred fifty years. Each title was carefully selected to "fit" the curricular needs of the undergraduate students. Augustana librarians took great pride in focused collection development. Faculty were confident that the students would be able to fulfill nearly all of their research needs by using the collections onsite. The books purchased were highly recommended for undergraduate education by *Choice, Books for College Libraries,* etc. and the library subscribed to the leading periodicals that were covered by the indexes we selected and owned. We often succeeded in our goal of supplying nearly full coverage of these indexes! Periodical titles were selected **with** the faculty, thereby insuring that our holdings supported the curriculum and that the faculty would be the primary "salespersons" of the collections. Students would still seek the path of least resistance, but the librarians and instructors would have built this path using carefully chosen high quality materials.

Today, we find ourselves struggling with the task of constructing this "path" in an electronic maze. Full text journals are sold in packages developed by the vendor/aggregator or publisher; inclusion of a title in these packages is driven primarily by contract negotiations and by volume (the more titles, the better). A selection process based on specific academic needs matters little to the vendors–nor could it, given the diverse libraries to which the packages are marketed. Not surprisingly, then, these journal packages include titles that have **not** been carefully selected for our curriculum and that sometimes are not wanted at all. Having invested in these full-text packages, we find ourselves managing "super-stores" of journal articles (ProQuest, Lexis/Nexis, InfoTrac, etc.) rather than the *small, tailored, stable* collection on which we prided ourselves in the past. And it is in these "super-stores"–many of which contain a large supply of popular news sources–that our inexperienced, hurried undergraduates will do their research.

Popular sources do have their purpose in an undergraduate collection. Students needing overview articles, a few facts for a short speech, or an examination of how the popular press is presenting an issue often have been directed to "trade" journals. But in the past, a liberal arts college never would subscribe to many of these because they did not meet the educational requirements of the college. Those that we owned were "separated" (as all paper subscriptions were) and their indexing was confined largely to one index, such as the *Readers' Guide to Periodical Literature* or *Academic Abstracts*. It was easy to describe to the inexperienced, eighteen-year-old student the difference between scholarly titles and popular titles because of the clear separation by indexing. Now we have an abundance of full text, both scholarly and popular, mixed together and linked to one index. A title by title–or, more accurately, article by article–examination is required to sort out the level of writing and reliability of the resource.

In addition, the permanence of electronic periodical "holdings" is far from assured. Titles appear and disappear–then sometimes reappear–with alarming frequency. The most immediate consequence of this situation is its effect on the quality of public service. When titles come and go on a daily or hourly basis, maintaining an accurate list of digital periodical holdings, either within or separate from the main catalog of library resources, is a nearly impossible job. When the student discovers that the holdings list is inaccurate and that the specific article so desperately needed is not immediately available, it is very irritating to her/him and embarrassing to the reference librarian! And if the student or a faculty member needs to check the same article a week or two later, it may no longer be part of the library's holdings because the publisher has altered its agreement with the vendor.

On the flip side of the disappearing journal problem is the duplication dilemma. Having purchased various journal packages from periodical aggregators, we often find ourselves subscribing to the same titles multiple times and/or in multiple formats. However, canceling a paper subscription in order to save money is a very risky venture. Discarding older paper or microform holdings in order to free up space or because they rarely are used might be downright foolhardy. If we are receiving more than one electronic "subscription" to a given journal, we usually have no choice at all: when the journal is part of two different packages and we need the titles unique to each one, we are stuck. In this world of insecure holdings and unwanted duplication, librarians at a liberal arts college must live with a nagging sense that they are being poor stewards of their very limited funds and with the frustration that no good alternative is available.

Tension #2: Bang for the Buck

In the late 1980's, many small colleges invested heavily in their collections, frequently spending nearly 6% of the institutional E & G (educational and general budget categories) in the library. These dollars were not nearly as large as a research institution, which meant that selection of materials was even more important; careful selection was essential to get the most "bang for the buck."

Now after nearly one hundred fifty years of collecting we find ourselves in several dilemmas. One of which is our huge backruns of periodical titles, many of which are untouched by human hands for years at a time. Do we relieve our crowded shelves? Do we continue to collect our longest title runs (and continue to bind them at even greater expense!) or do we trust the work of JSTOR and, soon, others to digitize and maintain backruns? Should we become the digitizers of our special "gems" (primary source materials) so they receive the same access as the full text services? Do we continue to subscribe to titles for current copy browsing when they will be available digitally within a month?

Rising costs and declining use of print journals make these decisions even more difficult. Since 1994, at Augustana College, print journal subscription costs have increased an average of 15% per year. During the same time, print journal usage has decreased nearly 49%. Print journals received a total of 15,884 uses in 1994-95, but this figure had decreased to 9,712 uses in 1998-99. When viewed in relation to total library materials use, the difference between print journal usage and electronic full text journal usage is even more startling; use of print journals in 1998-99 accounted for only 6% of total library material use, while electronic full-text usage had risen to 47% of total material use. (It is interesting to note that throughout this time period, book usage remained nearly constant at approximately 30% of total materials use. But will that change with the proliferation of e-books during the next few years?)

It is difficult to balance the wants of some of the faculty, who would rather see the College dollars go for print copy (as it was when they were students), with the desires of the students who prefer electronic formats. Most of our faculty are still judging the "worth" of the library by the titles (including backruns) on the shelf, yet students' research practices are dominated by electronic journals and other e-resources. So we currently sit in two worlds, desperately trying to balance the funding which has not grown enough to include all of the formats. It is reminiscent of the glacial move from the card catalog to the OPAC!

Another tension in this full-text world comes from the need to find on-going funding for the hardware and software needed to access and print the articles. The demand for faster CPU's, larger screens and better (even color) printers is unrelenting. We have found that at this point it is cheaper (both labor and supplies) to allow for free printing. We have yet to determine the breaking point in our budget if the use of the services increases. The question of whether we should consider the hardware as part of the acquisitions costs–like the binding of a book–is appearing on the horizon. One thing is clear: students will no longer photocopy hard copy unless they have no other choice. Why pay $.10 a page and spend 10 minutes at the photocopy machine when you could print it free?

Tension #3: The Competition

Liberal arts colleges have become increasingly competitive. "Marketing" and "branding" are terms that are commonly heard in administrative circles today–terms that were blasphemous in prestigious colleges twenty years ago. While the library's collection, measured in volumes and titles (as well as depth and breadth) used to be the marketing tool, today we are marketing our "wiredness." There is increasing pressure to offer the newest and the best of electronic services so that we will appeal to the student preparing for the future work world–a world that most of us cannot even imagine!

In this new competitive world, the student is the "customer" and the "customer" needs to be satisfied. A student selects a private small liberal arts school for its intimate community, a low teacher-student ratio, a close nurturing environment and a value-driven selection of scholarship support services. However, speed, efficiency and attractiveness are the seducers to the students. As the library fulfills its role in this supporting environment, it often seems like an oxymoron to emphasize speedy research.

Meanwhile, it also is difficult to watch our previously "unique" journal collections replicate those of our competitors. As we continue to find our best full-text economies in large package buys, we feel that we are losing our uniqueness. It is interesting that at many colleges, including Augustana, more and more attention is being given to the *special collections* and to their integration into the undergraduate education as well as their digitization. These resources are our uniqueness in the vendor driven world of full-text periodical packages.

Tension #4: The Consortia Scramble

The quirky pricing of electronic packages by the vendors has us all scrambling for the "best" deal which usually means joining the largest consortia we can find. In the state of Illinois, this means hoping that the "big" guys will stay with the State instead of putting their allegiance with their fellow research institutions, e.g., CIC, Big 12, etc. This gives the little guys (usually measured in terms of FTE) a larger pond to swim in. But loyalty holds no sway when we are all searching for the best price.

The complexities of consortia purchases and licensing as well as the scope and variety of digital journal packages make decision-making less than simple. For example, the Augustana Library recently received offers through two consortia; the product contained 75 journals with "module" options by subject or by publisher. Pricing was based on FTE and by number of schools participating. In order to make the decision, our duplicate print holdings and digital holdings (through another provider) and as well as our usage figures for both had to be checked. We also had to assess the value of the journals in this package that we did not hold in any form. If this product had not been announced and described in detail well before the consortia negotiations and if offers had not been entirely uniform from one consortium to another (a rare and wonderful thing in itself!), we would have had approximately one week or less in which to do all of our assessment and to compare one offer with another. Unfortunately, the one or two-week scramble and the need to compare the proverbial apple with the orange are far more common in the days of consortia purchases of digital periodical packages.

Tension #5: Disconnection with Faculty

The journal pricing inflation of the 1980s caused all of us to trim our journal collections to a lean and mean level. We did this in often-

painful discussions with the faculty. Each title was debated, priori-
tized, and justified by cost and worth. Now instead of purchasing a
few titles that represent the expressed request of a professor, we must
convince them that the consortia "buy" of a package is a better deal.
We have to debate the value of a package against the individual's
requested titles. Sometimes these requested titles are from small presses (never to be included in the aggregated packages) where a particular
teacher has published his/her paper or which represents a point of view
held dear by the faculty member. Economics are playing a stronger
role in the decision making process than the individual needs of a
professor. The faculty are no longer strong partners in the selection
process of journal titles.

   Faculty understand the cost of a journal subscription, although they
often express shock with the difference in cost between the library
subscription and their personal subscription to the same title. However, most faculty don't seem to grasp the issues related to full-text
periodicals–"Why do we have all of these digital titles that we have
not requested?" or, "Why do titles come and go from the database?"
There is much confusion about the Internet and what is on it as well as
which journals the library subscribes to through their own selection
versus what "packages" are available via other contractual agreements. Similarly, there is confusion about why some journals are
available from one's home (materials provided by State funds) and
why some are only available on campus. Most of the faculty don't
understand the concept of access vs. ownership and assume that it
must be cheaper (or even free) to access via the Internet than to own
paper subscriptions. From the perspective of the user, we have successfully erased the visible difference between licensed packages, subscription full-text titles, and "free" resources on the WEB–creating a
seamless interface to all electronic resources. While there is *no* reason
why our users should understand these complexities, this lack of understanding makes it very difficult to explain the budgetary and networking choices that need to be made.

   In the "paper-only" world of periodical collections, most liberal
arts colleges have added few if any journals in the past ten years. Now,
as a result of the aggregator packages, we have added many digital
journals and have not consulted the faculty about the value of the
titles. In fact, the librarians, who work with these digital packages
daily, can barely keep up with the titles to which we have access. We

could hardly expect the faculty to do so. And since we can't keep up with the many titles, we call these packages by their vendors' names: ProQuest Direct, Project Muse, Lexis/Nexis (or Lexis/Nexis UNIverse, or Academic Universe, or CIS Academic Universe, or whatever the latest name is!). Small wonder it is completely baffling to the faculty.

Browsing is, for many of our faculty, a long-held and beloved style of research–and it certainly does have educational value. Faculty hopes that the undergraduate students will keep up their reading of selected journals is probably too idealistic for all but the top students. However, browsing for possible paper topics or for "hot" issues in the field is *not* too much to hope for–it has a clear purpose for our hurried students. Faculty have played a key role in promoting certain journal titles to their students for this browsing purpose. In addition, faculty have a long-held and beloved experience of the library as a building which holds journals they can touch, and they resist the trend away from this. Students, on the other hand, prefer to sit at the computer to browse the keywords and titles for that paper topic.

All of this results in a kind of "disconnect" between faculty and librarians and students. This may result in more appreciation for librarians, but may also result in their seeing us even more as bureaucrats and/or technicians. Either way, there is an undesirable separation.

Tension #6:
The "Sage on the Stage" or "Guide on the Side" Anxieties

The number of librarians in the college libraries has not grown in proportion to the new body of electronic material.[6] In fact, a ten-year view of the Oberlin Group of liberal arts colleges[7] shows that the average number of librarians employed has not increased at all. Most librarians continue to spend the majority of their time in direct service (reference desk, library instruction, faculty liaison work and campus governance) and in traditional development of the collections. The electronic resources are an add-on responsibility without the other responsibilities being diminished. Many unfamiliar titles that are included in the aggregate packages need to be reviewed to determine if retrospective coverage is available or if the scholarship of the articles is such that it should be recommended to the students. Decisions about duplicating print subscriptions, the value of advertising and graphics to the research and the value of the current browsing collection titles must be investigated on a title by title basis. This takes an enormous amount of time. It is difficult to "let go" of the role of "information expert" and become the facilitator or guide as the literature tells us to do. Many of our faculty do not have the time to spend hours searching and evaluating the new resources. They have traditionally looked to the librarians for that support. We, the librarians, are afraid that we are not meeting the call as we have prided ourselves in doing in the past.

Without constant contact with the daily ins and outs of consortia, licenses, and vendor buyouts, there is little hope that every librarian will have a full understanding of the issues that affect the quality and costs of digital full-text journals. Robert Galbreath said that " . . . with the number and complexity of issues involved in adding electronic resources, we have found that we need a combination of talents to make informed decisions: the subject specialist, the electronic information specialist, the systems librarian and input from reference and serials."[8] At the small liberal arts college, one or two librarians, who continue to carry the same workload as they did ten years ago, must provide this mix of "talents."

Remember when an acrobat used to be a guy who swung on a trapeze at the circus? Well, the acrobat is now a text "reader"! Explaining that to an older faculty member is just one of the many technical stunts required from the librarian at the reference desk. "Why is this full text loading so slowly?" "How do I print from this database and why is it different from the last one?" There is a technical knowledge/expertise that is expected at the moment of assistance. When a resource is not working, the librarian must determine if there is a difficulty with the resource server or with our network connection or with our own server or with this particular computer. Working on all of the technical matters (and breakdowns) takes a great deal of time away from the real, important work of librarianship.

And lastly, with today's user-friendly databases and with remote access to the library resources, fewer students request assistance in the library. The question "which key do I punch?" used to be the librarians' chance to gain entrée to the student's topic selection, search strategy, etc. The process of limiting or reviewing interlibrary loan requests provided yet another opportunity for the librarian to discuss research strategy with the student. The technological move to unmediated interlibrary loan requests has further distanced the librarian from the "teachable moment" with a student, albeit making the process easier and faster.

Tension #7: At the Speed of Lightning . . .

Our traditional age students are the cell phone/MP3/sound-bite/computer-loving generation. They don't remember a world without these things. There are expectations of immediate gratification and entitlement.

Five years ago, if asked during a library instruction session, a sizeable number of students would say that they had rarely used an electronic index. When we ask today, we find that about the same number of students have never used a paper index! As high school students, they have been accustomed to doing their research through AOL and expect the same colorful, packaged information that they found on the commercial sites (complete with advertising!). They expect their research strategies to be woven around hypertext links so that the entire process of research and formation of their bibliographies can be completed at a single session at the computer. The new free Encyclopedia Britannica online will probably increase this trend.

To slow down these speedy students, many faculty have set up barriers such as "no WEB resources for this paper." This is perhaps an artificial barrier intended to provide students with an experience of doing research the old-fashioned way, "the way I had to do research." But more importantly, fears of the declining quality of resources used by students and fears that students do not have the skills to evaluate resources, as evidenced by the widespread interest in information literacy programs, have led to this prescribed method of bibliography–not unlike the writing assignments requiring five books, five journals, five government documents, etc. In the library, we are searching for those tags which will clue students which resources are considered scholarly and which are trade–tags (authorship, publisher, editorial board, etc.) that can be interpreted for evaluation of e-resources like we have for print materials. Rather than restrict the resources, we should teach students and faculty how to evaluate and select quality information self-sufficiently. Is there an underlying assumption that the electronic publishing world will stabilize and standardize like the print world? One thing is a reality: today's students will not stand for artificial barriers or a "behind the times" library.

CONCLUSION

As we look at the Augustana College Library experience and search for ways to refocus our library services to lessen these tensions, certain directions come to mind:

- Take a stronger role with the vendors to ensure that our electronic collections remain focused and of a quality for the undergraduate education.
- Let go of some of our traditional expenses so we can reallocate funds to full-text collections.
- Use student outcomes to "market" our institution rather than using the "things" we can count.
- Take comfort in knowing that the quirky pricing of full-text journals will be standardized when the vendors and/or scholars find a model that satisfies their wants and needs (perhaps when we all belong to the "world of libraries" consortia).
- Work with the faculty to integrate "information literacy" outcomes into the curricular program.
- Revisit the value of browsing and find new ways to encourage our students to appreciate the serendipity of discovery in both electronic and print resources.
- Level the playing field between faculty and between faculty and students in terms of computer fluency.

These directions are broad and will only partially relieve the tensions that are being talked and written about in all library circles. Misery loves company; it is always gratifying to know that all libraries, large and small, public and private, share some if not all of these stresses. But, we all need to accept these tensions, learn from these tensions and even thrive on these tensions.

Perhaps the greatest cause of stress is the expectation that there will be an end to these transitions, and libraries will reach a state of utopian stability. In her paper *Border Crossings: Strengthening Collaboration for Meaningful Student Inquiry* (given at the ACM Bibliographic Instruction Conference, Oct. 22, 1998), Barbara Fister described our current situation in librarianship:

A second sort of border that is on everyone's mind these days is the border between print and electronic technologies. This electronic frontier occupies a lot of our attention and energy, and it has in many ways complicated our lives as well as enriched them. . . . I think at times we are all inclined to view ourselves as forward thinking techies *or* as people of the book. We may consider ourselves one or the other at different hours of the very same day. We are neither of those things, and both. . . . We are people of a distinct hybrid culture. . . . Although the fluidity of this culture and the constancy of change makes us think we are crossing a frontier, on our way to a new and different place as yet unknown, losing one culture as we are dominated by the other, in fact we are going to be in this hybrid place for a long, long time."

As we live in this hybrid culture, we need to focus on the desired outcomes of a liberal arts education and the role the library plays in this educational process. Our tools may be constantly changing but the product remains the same and is consistent with the college mission we have worked with for over one hundred fifty years. At Augustana College that is to offer "a challenging education that develops qualities of mind and spirit necessary for a rewarding life of leadership and service in a diverse and changing world."

> *Candide's descendants survey their gardens and long for the day when things will settle down. Someday, we think, we will be in control again and stop feeling so many tensions. But is it this very longing which creates much of the tension? This is not a transition that will be accomplished in the foreseeable future and after which we will live in a more peaceful, manageable place. This is it: this confusing but fascinating mixture of resources* is *our garden–which, like the rest of life, continues to grow while we are making other plans. We must stop longing for perfection (whether in the future or the imaginary past), and, like the original Candide, cultivate our garden.*

NOTES

1. Van Dam, S. & DiMarco, S.R. (1998). Full text document delivery: A study understanding user perceptions and needs. *Journal of Interlibrary Loan, Document Delivery & Information Supply, 9*(1), 83-103.

2. Galbreath, R. (1997) Nailing jell-o to the wall? Collection management in the electronic era. *North Carolina Libraries, 50*, 18-21.

3. Buckland, M. (1995). What will collection developers do? *Information Technology and Libraries, 14*, 155-59.

4. LaGuardia, C. (1995). Virtual dreams give way to digital reality. *Library Journal, 120*, 42-44.

5. Lougee, W. (1995) Beyond access: new concepts, new tensions for collection development in a digital environment. *Collection Building, 14*(3), 19-25.

6. For an excellent analysis of these problems See: Seiden, P. (1997) Restructuring liberal arts college libraries: Seven organizational strategies. In C. Schwartz (Ed.), *Restructuring academic libraries.* Chicago: Association of College & Research Libraries.

7. Oberlin Group Statistics from 1990 to 1998.

8. Galbreath, 19.

9. Fister, B. (1998). Border crossings: Strengthening collaboration for meaningful student inquiry. Paper presented at the ACM Bibliographic Instruction Conference, St. Olaf College.

Information Technology and Collection Development Departments in the Academic Library: Striving to Reach a Common Understanding

David C. Fowler

INTRODUCTION

Electronic resources are becoming an increasingly common and pervasive presence and influence in libraries of all types, but they have become especially so in academic libraries. Many scientific, technical, medical, and other academic journals are also being released in electronic editions, in addition to the paper versions, as well as the many free and for-fee full-text and bibliographic databases that are now available. This has made making well-informed collection development decisions based on the evaluation of technical issues involved, in addition to their selection, purchase and mounting, an indispensable function in the library. This function now requires very close cooperation between collection development personnel, including the subject bibliographers, the information technology (or systems) department, and the electronic resources coordinator, if one is available. Relationships between the information technology and collection development departments in modern academic libraries are complex and evolving, and will probably continue to be so for the foreseeable future. This relationship can be characterized as involving two organizations that

[Haworth co-indexing entry note]: "Information Technology and Collection Development Departments in the Academic Library: Striving to Reach a Common Understanding." Fowler, David C. Co-published simultaneously in *Collection Management* (The Haworth Information Press, an imprint of The Haworth Press, Inc.) Vol. 25, No. 1/2, 2000, pp. 17-36; and: *Electronic Collection Management* (ed: Suzan D. McGinnis) The Haworth Information Press, an imprint of The Haworth Press, Inc., 2000, pp. 17-36. Single or multiple copies of this article are available for a fee from The Haworth Document Delivery Service [1-800-342-9678, 9:00 a.m. - 5:00 p.m. (EST). E-mail address: getinfo@haworthpressinc.com].

speak somewhat different languages, and which are likely to have somewhat different priorities, but that must nonetheless struggle and persevere to reach a mutual understanding of each other, and of their common goals, so as to best serve the end-users in the university community–the students, faculty and staff.

The relationship between the collection development and information technology departments possesses a number of characteristics and issues that will be described and discussed herein, including:

- Including the information technology department in collection development decisions from the start, so that technical ramifications can be made clear to collection development personnel, and so that any difficult issues can be assessed and dealt with at the front-end of the process, and not, as sometimes happens, at the end.
- Allowing the information technology department to better educate collection development personnel, so that they can better understand the technologies involved in today's electronic library, including hardware platforms, appropriate software and the authentication process.
- Allowing the collection development staff a voice in conducting long-term strategic planning for the information technology department, so that IT personnel can better understand the types of electronic products being evaluated by their institution, and allowing IT personnel a voice in collection development planning as well. This allows collection development personnel to likewise understand where current trends in technology are driving the electronic products that are being marketed to electronic libraries.
- Developing a common IT-CD understanding on the types of statistics being requested and required of electronic products by the collection development department, and by library administration, so that the IT department can tailor and interrogate library software packages accordingly, and so that similar report requirements can be accurately requested of other electronic product vendors.
- Developing a common goal of developing electronic products for the public service area that behave in the most user-friendly manner possible. Also, both groups need to work to make interfaces

usable and understandable, which includes eliminating unnecessary intermediate screens, making access as fast as possible, and
making the process of access intuitive, and not problematic for
the patron.
• Finally, utilizing a staff member as a full-time or collateral-duty
"electronic resources coordinator" to help facilitating the inter-
facing of these two staff groups, as well as with the acquisitions
department and their contacts as pertaining to electronic resources, with vendors and faculty.

BRINGING IN THE IT DEPARTMENT EARLY

A common difficulty in fostering cooperation and understanding
between two organizations with differing professional languages is
that when both are required to bring about the successful completion
of a common project, is that one of the groups may not be brought in
until it is prohibitively late in the process for it to bring some of its
collective talents and abilities to bear. As a result, mistakes that may
have been avoided are not; Insights that might have been valuable at
an earlier date are less useful; Expenses that could have been avoided
if both units brought their diverse talents to play at an earlier stage are
not avoided. Much like the arguments that decry the waste of talent to
a society, when a large group of individuals (for instance, women) is
denied full access to the workforce, a similar argument could be made
that says that an organization is foolishly squandering its already paid
and available talent by not bringing all of its relevant personnel on-
board to solve problems and to assist in planning for future operations.
The people are there–so why not use them?

Thus, if one unit of an organization (and in this situation, it will be
posited as being a library collection development department) assumes that it can evaluate, research and solve all problems that it faces
about acquiring, implementing and trouble-shooting electronic resources in a vacuum, it will undoubtedly be making a serious mistake.
The collection development department, while undoubtedly consisting
of a group of intelligent and able individuals, does not have a monopo-
ly on all knowledge in this arena. Indeed, it would not be uncommon
for technical and basic "hardware" knowledge to be lacking in some
degree for this group of library professionals. This is not meant to be a
slight on them–it is just that they bring other abilities to the table for

the accomplishment of the library mission. Consequently, it is always going to be an excellent idea to bring in one or more persons from the IT department to help to fully develop and to fully understand the advantages and disadvantages of any electronic product that a library is proposing to acquire.

A collection development officer may know that he or she likes and wants a product, but may be wasting his or her time, if they proceed with a purchase before they find the answers to several important questions that only the IT department is likely to have the knowledge to answer. Kaag has listed several important issues that must be considered before a product can proceed to fruition, including:

- The resource needs to meet networking standards, even if financial or legal constraints limit the initial networking of it.
- The resource needs to meet international data standards.
- Multiple simultaneous use agreements are preferable.
- When competing products are comparable in terms of cost, preference is given to the product that does not include added networking charges.
- Preferring products that enhance existing access, or that maximize the use of existing resources.[1] The IT department can help immeasurably with examining these issues, and the wise collection development person will know (and will hopefully feel comfortable in doing so) when to go to their friendly computer expert for these answers.

The information technology department will bring to the table expertise on computer hardware and software, and the common problems that accompany these. In particular, some of the most useful knowledge that it can introduce to the discussion includes questions about IP ranges, remote access, firewalls, passwords and scripting. In other words, no electronic resource will work well, or work at all, unless technical issues have been identified and addressed. The sooner these issues are addressed and either given a go-ahead, or had their particular pressing problems solved, the sooner a project can go forward to the benefit of all. To wait until the end of the process to vet an electronic resource for obstacles is simply sheer folly. It is far better to bring the in-house experts in early to head off serious problems later.

In terms of examples, the IT department is going to be skilled in anticipating and recognizing problem or "gray" areas in electronic products, for instance, those with rolling five-year accumulations, that lose the oldest year indexed, once the newest year comes online. Sometimes this feature is not always obvious, so an IT person may know what to look for, and will also know to ask if an online supplement is available elsewhere in whole or in part for the portion that the library will be losing. IT professionals can also assist in writing the technical standards for collection development policies so that future problems can be anticipated and avoided, such as equipment compatibility, frequency of updating and others. They will understand if locally mounted resources will work well, or at all, with the existing OPAC interface. They know to ask if there is any kind of enhanced access, and if that will cost more. Also, they will be able to tell the collection development department what, if any, additional hardware and software will be required, and their associated costs. Other questions that they can answer for the CD staff include: what networking requirements are, systems maintenance costs and requirements, the memory space required for the system to operate, and so on.[2]

Many experienced subject selectors may feel quite comfortable dealing with electronic products, but networking brings a whole other dimension to the table, and even they may feel out of their depth. This is why Davis states that "The selector must rely on advice and reliable testing from the technical staff to assure the product will sustain the desired number of network users without a significant drop in response time.[3]

While the author is trying not to generalize too much, it is probably fair to say that most collection development personnel would not know how many slots are available on their network server; how one goes about scripting FirstSearch authorizations correctly, what special arrangements need to be made for remote access to work seamlessly and so on. Bringing in the IT department gets this expertise, and issues such as these examined at an early, and more logical opportunity.

HOW THE IT DEPARTMENT CAN EDUCATE THE LIBRARY

Along the lines already discussed, it would make excellent sense for a library to establish a policy for the IT department to regularly disseminate current and relevant information applicable to the collection development process, and to the public service arena to the very people involved in making such decisions, and also to perhaps hold formal training sessions at regular intervals to educate the CD staff (and others) on library computing issues. A large proportion of the non-technical staff at any given library will likely have varying levels of limited knowledge on the computing systems that make the library operate. This is most likely because there is no everyday need for these personnel to utilize such information. In other words, if you don't deal with it daily, you probably tend to put it out of your mind, and place a certain amount of faith in the IT staff working behind the scenes to keep the library's computers and servers running for you. As long as these things are running smoothly, many will feel that this arrangement is just fine.

This may be okay, so far as it goes, but the day will come for most any librarian when they will need more information on just how things operate in the computer room, or in the CD-ROM tower. Having the IT staff available to answer questions is a great resource to have, but the IT department could also be more proactive in their outreach efforts, and instead of waiting for the library to come to them for information, they could develop a program to bring the information to the library.

This has at least three compelling advantages: One is that it will better educate the collection development staff and other library staff on computing and electronic resources issues; Another is that such education may help "cut off at the pass" a potential developing problem, by arming non-computing staff with the knowledge to recognize potential technical difficulties in the public service area before they become really serious problems; Finally, such outreach will simply give the often-invisible computing staff a little bit of a higher profile in the library. People in the public service area will begin to recognize faces and personalities that they can approach for future assistance, and to ask questions of. It also never hurts to engage in a bit of self-promotion for one's department, either!

Of course, not every morsel of knowledge that the IT staff attempts to impart will stick, but some of it may, and with periodic reinforcement, even more of it will. For the part of the collection development staff, it could be an empowering experience to begin to understand some of the "black arts" of computing.

GIVING EACH OTHER A VOICE

Another step towards getting each other involved in each others' processes is to, when appropriate, invite representatives from the other department to each others' meetings, especially when policy is being discussed in the CD department that will affect the IT department, and vice versa. Absent this, it is likely that meetings dealing with electronic resources, and their associated problems and difficulties, will be reactive in nature, rather than taking a more proactive approach. This also holds true when conducting strategic planning for electronic resources. Everyone at one point or another probably feels like they have more than enough meetings to attend on any given week, but the potential value of having one person from the other department sit in on, and contribute to deliberations about issues that affect both areas is great. These two illustrative examples may be helpful in illustrating this:

Example A: The information technology department is in the process of redesigning the library webpages.

The IT department, and in particular, the webmaster have the responsibility for the style and organization of these pages. One option would be for the IT department to execute this responsibility unilaterally. Perhaps the webmaster would come up with a number of possible looks and designs for the pages, and have them approved by the head of the IT department, probably with the library director's consent. Assuming that you have a talented and creative webmaster, this might be a fine way to proceed if the options presented by him or her are met with agreement by all parties. However, it would probably be a better idea to form a committee or task force to explore the issue of redesigning the library web, to include the webmaster and perhaps other representatives of the IT department. However, this notional committee should also include the collections officer, the electronic resources coordinator and some subject area bibliographers; If there is a separate reference staff, it would be essential to include some of these members as well. The reason for this is clear: The IT department has relatively little contact with the end-user community–the faculty, staff and students of the university who are in the reference area, using the computers and the library webpages. It is unsurprising that they might have only limited ideas of what functions the users were utilizing, and what features they liked, and which they disliked. On the other hand, the reference and collection development staff are the front-line forces of the library in terms of working with the public, and in terms of faculty contact. These personnel would have unparalleled insights based on experience, on what products the end-users are utilizing and what features and services they are expecting and demanding that the library provide. It only makes sense to include them in this discussion as well. The entire deliberative process will be strengthened by the participation of a diverse group with differing strengths and insights on what needs to be done. The end result will undoubtedly display the results of this combined effort, and a stronger and more responsive product will be produced.

Example B: The collection development department is in the process of migrating a particular database from a CD-ROM platform to an online product. There is a complicated license involved specifying the number of users and conditions for downloading copies, interlibrary loan and linking to class webpages. Further, the technical requirements are headache inducing, with questions being raised about the feasibility of providing remote access, and about the scripting of authorizations for the database. Even if the collection development staff has some knowledge of some of these issues, it makes little sense for them to bump around in the dark by themselves with their flashlight working only intermittently, when there are in-house experts available, who can provide much greater illumination on the subject. As in Example A, the better way to go, would be to bring in one or more members of the IT department to help examine and resolve technical issues in an assured and knowledgeable manner. The IT department will know what is and what is not possible to accomplish given the hardware available at the library, and given the software being offered for its use. They can serve as an auxiliary resource, along with an electronic resources coordinator in assessing some of the technical aspects of the license being considered as well.

In addition to specific single-product examples such as these, it only makes sense that both departments be involved in any conversations about long-range strategic planning for the library that will involve issues affecting both groups, and which will require the expertise of both departments. It has been said that electronic resources have contributed to a gradual blurring of the lines, if not a lowering of some of the barriers between the public service and technical service divisions of libraries. It would not be a surprise then, if the same factors also contributed to a lowering of barriers between the information technology/systems community and the rest of the library, in particular, the collection development personnel.

Collection development personnel should realize that the IT department will usually have the capability of building an electronic infrastructure that will meet the needs of the public service area. The IT department will make sure that network routing and wiring is in place; they will make sure that the network interface can anticipate traffic loads, and so on. Also, the IT department will take a holistic view, and look at not just the technology that the library has in place, but at what the rest of the campus will support. Great electronic databases will lose a lot of their luster if they can be accessed at the library, but not in computer labs, or on the faculty's desktops. Regardless, collection development will need to let the IT department know very clearly *what* they need and want to make available to the library users.

Sometimes bringing two different groups together (such as librarians and computing professionals) can be a difficult task, and lowering the aforementioned barriers can be difficult. The difficulty in this case can best be described as a cultural one. Hirshon describes this as primarily being a reflection of the two groups' approaches to problem solving, in part brought about by the traditional gender biases of these professions. Although these biases are not as remarkable as they once were, significant vestiges still remain. Hirshon illustrates this by describing information technology professionals as predominantly male, and librarians as predominantly female. Building on this, he states that the IT professionals had a "'traditional' client base often consist(ing) of engineers and scientists who were technologically literate and engaged," and as a result, IT personnel thus "most enjoy helping those who are able to help themselves." By contrast, the traditionally female librarian population "approach client services from a nurturing and instructional mode; they want to guide and mentor, working especially well with neophytes. . . ."[4] Thus, the languages that library and computer personnel use to solve problems probably comes into conflict when they attempt to communicate in general, and in particular, when they work to solve problems that start in one area, but end up in the other. Collection development personnel may know there is a problem, but may not know how to describe it in terms that the IT staff can use to narrow down the possible root causes. Conversely, IT personnel, who may come from a completely non-library background, may be focused on solving the problem, but may not be able to ask the questions in terms that allow the collection development staff to be most helpful.

While there are no quick answers, allowing each other to participate in each other's planning and to have a voice in each other's world, will go a long way to lowering the increasingly artificial barriers that keep the two departments apart–barriers which more and more, serve no useful purpose in the library.

REPORTS AND STATISTICS

Modern libraries are becoming more and more reliant on all varieties of statistics: personnel statistics, financial statistics, acquisition statistics, user statistics, web statistics, and so the list continues. In this respect, libraries are becoming more and more like the corporate world. In order to best justify their existence, library directors need supporting materials to advance and protect library interests. This support frequently comes in the form of statistical materials gathered from various sources. User statistics are especially important, so that a library administrator can say that "x" number of bodies passed through the doors, or "y" number of books were circulated during the most recent fiscal year.

Additionally, such statistics are an opportunity to provide a wealth of information on the usage of library resources to the collection development staff, which can be used during selection or de-selection (weeding) decisions. Knowing how often a resource is looked at, requested or downloaded can provide important insights to what the library's patrons are interested in, in terms of electronic resources. In cases where the electronic version has a print companion, it may also be possible to make inferences about the usage of the print as well. Of course, from the vendor's point-of-view, this sometimes can be a double-edged sword, and consequently they may balk at providing all statistics requested, for fear that little-used publications will be cut.

With electronic resources now arriving at the forefront of library operations, there exists a new opportunity for statistical data to be gathered on their usage (or not), on the number of times they have been accessed (or not) and breaking out which titles in aggregator databases are being used the most often, and so on. This is where it is important for the IT department to become involved, as they will be the best resource to know what information can and cannot be extracted from online resources, and also so as to query their counterparts at the vendor's technical office to find this out. They will also be the primary resource, on how to get the most out of the library Web-

PACs and StaffPACs, and which may be able to be used for statistical extraction for electronic resources that are accessed off of the library webpages. Collection development personnel will need to bring in IT up front, so that they can get a handle on the CD department's specific statistical needs. IT will be far less effective if they have only general requests for statistics. Different statistical data needs to be accessed in different ways, and from different sources, depending on whether or not it is a networked resource, and remotely-accessed resource, a single-work station resource, and so on. In addition, certain resources may be shared among institutions, and within consortia, and agreements on what data is needed, and from where to get it will need to be established by the IT department. Once again, this illustrates the absolute necessity for collection development and information technology personnel to be working together on issues such as these. The collection development department (and library administration) have a definite need for such information, so that knowledgeable decisions can be made about library operations and resources, and the local IT department is in a unique position to provide, or to facilitate the delivery of that information. Vital information such as this may go unutilized, or un-accessed without their assistance. Communication between the two groups is once again important, so that needs and results can be properly transmitted to and from both groups.

DOES IT MAKE SENSE TO THE PATRONS?

Sometimes in our zeal to get new products out to the patron, we sometimes forget to do a "compass check" as to whether or not the resources that we are placing out there for people to use and enjoy make sense to the public, and further, one being presented in a clear and logical way that the public readily understands. Sometimes collection development officers spend a lot of time on making sure that the former is true, but let the latter issue remain somewhat wanting. However, having excellent resources available will do little good, if patrons get lost as they wander around your website looking for them, especially if it is a confusing and poorly organized website with unclear navigational features.

This is another area where the two departments can meet to reach a common understanding of what is required, and what is desired. What is required is a well-laid out and clearly organized library website with a good searching facility that is easy to use. What is desired is to make it look aesthetically pleasing, with maybe a dash of pizzazz that makes it interesting to look at. These two factors combined should make a website that users will enjoy and appreciate coming back to use again and again. The information technology department's strength will be in conducting physical (or perhaps virtual) construction of the site, setting up the linkages, the layout, and taking care of assorted technical considerations. On the other hand, the collection development and public service personnel will have their greatest strengths on display as they help design *how* materials are displayed, and *what* content is presented. Their daily interaction with students and faculty will give them the required insights into knowing not only what people expect to find on the site, but *where* they would logically expect it to be. This will include organizing all electronic resources into logical subject areas (and often into more than just one), or into types of resources (indexes, e-journals, e-books), making decisions of when/how to break down the content of aggregator databases into more useful subheadings, when to make linkages and cross-references to and from these resources and the catalog records, between subject pages and banner pages and others.

The collection development people will know better than anyone else what the faculty are looking for as they pursue their research, and can be in an indispensable position to know how to put together a page on particle physics resources, or veterinary journals, or literary weblinks, or any number of other subject areas.

They will be best at knowing where resources should logically belong and where their audience will be looking for them. They should also consider that if a particular database has low usage statistics, that this may be linked to a particularly poorly thought-out location on the library web. Perhaps shifting its location will improve that problem.

In addition, our two areas will need to communicate in regards to what is the best and most consistent way to develop the "behind the curtain" parts of the presentation. For instance, will password access be allowed, or will IP address registration only be pursued? If collection development needs resources on the web that will require passwords, then they will need to consult with IT on the best and most secure method to store them, so that they will be as readily available as possible to those who need to use them, but also not too "exposed" to members of the general public who the vendor does not want access granted to. When a webpage exists that has a number of intermediate screens (such as a "Welcome" page), decisions need to be made if a link will be made only to the main page, or also to some of its sub-pages as well, some of which might have more precise and advantageous subject-specific coverage.

The goal will be for the IT and collection development departments to develop a webpage and searching apparatus that will be as clear and as intuitive to the user as possible. In order to do this successfully, the CD staff will need to have a clear knowledge of what is technologically possible, and the IT staff will need to have an accurate picture of user needs and expectations.

AN ELECTRONIC RESOURCES COORDINATOR

One challenging aspect of making two diverse groups of personnel in a library come together and cooperate, even though their respective "corporate cultures" may be quite different, is to find a central hub to which the two departments can interact through on matters of mutual interest. One solution, and the solution that Iowa State University has taken, is to appoint an individual as an "electronic resources coordinator." In the case of Iowa State, the individual in that position engages in this work in a full-time manner. For smaller institutions, however, it may be more practical to have an individual employed in another position in the library, work as an ERC in a part-time or "collateral duty" capacity.

Prior to the hiring of a full-time ERC in early 1999, Iowa State employed a humanities cataloger/collection development librarian as the de facto (one-third time) electronic resources coordinator, but it soon proved to be that the requirements of attending to electronic resources questions at this university were outstripping the capabilities of a person holding only a part-time position, so in 1998 it was decided to create a new position to handle these questions, and that this position would be located within the acquisitions department, in the technical services division. Importantly, this position was not located in either the IT department or in the collection development department, allowing the individual in this position a certain freedom from parochial entanglements in those areas. This allowed the electronic resources coordinator to address concerns from both arenas with at least a modicum of impartiality, and to also serve as a common communication focal point when dealing with vendors.

Within this basic framework, the author was hired to fill this position in early 1999, and has found the continual intermingling between the two worlds, as well as that of the acquisitions department, and also the vendor contact to be challenging and interesting work. Some of the challenges for an electronic resources coordinator is to know the languages and concerns of both corners, and to be reasonably fluent enough in both of them so as to be able to relate to each other's concerns in terms that they can both understand. In the electronic resources coordinator's role as an acquisitions department staff member, these contacts also serve as valuable sources of information when dealing with matters that impact on his or her own department. The electronic resources coordinator after all, has that "third foot" in the technical services world as well. It would even be fair to say that relations with the cataloging section (though organizationally a part of technical services), would constitute a "fourth foot" as well, as catalogers and acquisitions specialists have fundamentally different job responsibilities.

The electronic resources coordinator can also serve as the focal point for users' questions on library database issues. This way if problems crop up, the ERC can triage them, and make a determination on whether or not he or she can fix it, or if the vendor needs to be contacted, or if there is simply a cataloging problem. The ERC will also know when to send a particularly difficult technical problem to the IT department. For example, the author once received a complaint from a faculty member that he was no longer able to access a certain chemistry database. Initially, there seemed to be no good reason for this, as the library's account was up-to-date, and Internet connections were working fine. A call to the vendor was most useful, eliminating several possibilities, until it was realized that the product had recently upgraded to a newer version, and all support for the older version had been withdrawn, without the library knowing about it. Once this was determined, the author then was able to give the IT department a specific problem with a known solution to fix it, rather than an unknown and undefined access problem.

In addition to standard queries at the reference desk, if a library possesses an electronic reference service, any questions that regard electronic products should likewise be routed to the ERC for action,

FIGURE 1. The Electronic Resources Coordinator

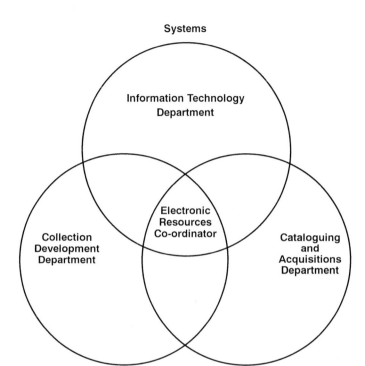

Systems

Information Technology
Department

Electronic
Resources
Co-ordinator

Collection
Development
Department

Cataloguing
and
Acquisitions
Department

Public   Technical Services

who can then reply directly to the patron when a solution is found. In this way, the electronic resources coordinator will be a common face for all to see when an electronic problem arises. The ERC will not be able to solve *all* of the problems, but he or she will be able to find the party that can solve it.

The responsibilities of this job, taken from the official Iowa State University position responsibilities statement, are described as follows:

Works collaboratively with the Acquisitions Department Head and Collections Officer, as well as the Electronic Resources Cataloging Coordinator, bibliographers, vendors, and the staff of the Information Technology Division to develop goals and strategies to acquire and manage electronic resources, and to assist in implementing those goals and strategies. Manages and coordinates the ordering and renewal of electronic resources. Coordinates the analysis of technical specifications, contract criteria, in particular licensing issues, and other business arrangements. In consultation with the Collections Officer, maintains license agreements and files and assures public access and current access to library electronic resources. Coordinates with the Cataloging Coordinator to assure public access and good record maintenance. Arranges for the testing of electronic resources and communicates effectively with the appropriate staff on these issues. Maintains currency in emerging issues in the acquisition of electronic resources and works with library groups that are considering issues related to electronic resources. Fosters and supports a collaborative approach to problem solving and decision making, with emphasis on facilitating and providing resources.[5]

This description sums up the depth and breadth of responsibilities of the job. To be successful, the electronic resources coordinator must be able to be flexible and adaptable to change. He or she must be able to communicate effectively with parties in three different departments; be able to articulate the views and needs of the collection development department to the IT department, and the requirements of the IT department to the collection development department. In essence, the electronic resources coordinator is the traffic cop, counselor and facilitator at the intersection of this two- or three-way street.

To illustrate the way the position works at Iowa State, is that for instance a subject bibliographer in the collection development department will become aware of a certain electronic database that would benefit his or her area. After conducting some basic research on the product, and determining that the cost will be acceptable, he or she will then fill out an "electronic serials orders form." This form details vital information that the electronic resources coordinator will need, such as title, vendor, vendor contact, and vendor address; also whether or not it is a trial or permanent addition, and whether or not it is an "add-on" to an existing print product. Other important data on the form include: price, subject code and subject coverage, ISSN (if one exists), the nature of the material (full-text, abstracts, table of contents), the format (online or CD-ROM), how accessed (web, library network, stand-alone), whether or not there are any restrictions, if

there are any special licensing issues and also any consortial arrangements involved. Once all of this information is determined to the best
of the subject bibliographer's knowledge, this form then proceeds to
the technical services division, where it arrives on the electronic resources coordinator's desk.

In the electronic resources coordinator's office, several things will
happen: The order form will be inspected to ensure that no vital
information is missing. The quality of the information on the form will
vary widely from bibliographer to bibliographer. Many are comfortable researching electronic products, and have little or no difficulty in
locating necessary technical and purchasing information for them.
Others have made the leap to cyberspace with more difficulty, and will
depend on the electronic resources coordinator to do the bulk of the
research work. In any case, depending on the completeness of the
form, the electronic resources coordinator may have to do additional
research on the product, with an eye on making sure a number of
things about it are workable in his or her library's environment. These
include:

- Inspecting the license for objectionable provisions, such as unacceptable interlibrary loan (ILL) restrictions, restrictions to off-
  campus usage by the university community, restrictions on dual-
  ownership sites on campus (such as government labs),
  unacceptable usage monitoring provisions and the location of the
  jurisdiction that any matters in dispute are to be resolved. Once
  the license is approved, it must be signed and returned to the vendor. In many cases, however, "point and click" licenses are being mounted on vendors' websites, which though easy and convenient, require extra vigilance, as the ease of clicking on the "I
  Agree" button on the screen before thoroughly reading all provisions can be enticing.
- Confirming that technical provisions are workable in your library
  environment. This often requires some important input from the
  information technology department, in order to confirm that the
  vendor's requirements are compatible with the library's requirements. In cases where the technical problems are becoming a
  huge ordeal, the electronic resources coordinator will need to
  know when it is time to let the library IT people start communicating with the vendor IT people, as there are times when the

contacts and negotiations need to be moved up to that technical level before anything else with the contract can proceed.

- For Internet products, the electronic resources coordinator must verify that the product can be accessed not only from workstations in and around the library, but also at other campus locations as well. Most vendors will now allow access to a fair number of IP range addresses for a campus network, but a few still insist on making it complicated, allowing only a certain number of a certain class of subnet addresses, or even allowing you to set up only one IP address (not even a range) at the time of registration. This is another area that may require assistance from the IT department.

- In cases where special authorizations must be scripted in order to allow campus access to the product, the IT department's involvement will be absolutely essential, as they have the expertise to get this done.

- Decisions need to be made on allowing password access, and the logistical headaches that instigates in terms of where to store them, what passwords and user IDs to use, etc., or instead adhering to an IP range-only policy.

- Information on the product is sent by the electronic resources coordinator to the serials cataloging section (or in some cases, to the monograph cataloging section), where a full cataloging record for the electronic product will be created. When the product is being locally mounted and/or networked, cataloging will also have to work with the IT department on the product's web placement, so a link can be created for the final record.

- The webmaster (located in the information technology department) will create a descriptive banner page, with links *to* the electronic product, and *from* one or more subject or other descriptive pages on the library web. The bibliographer (in the collection development department) who initiated the purchase is responsible for writing the actual description of the product, and transmitting it to the webmaster.

- Information technology personnel will usually be responsible for the final mounting of the database on the library web. When this process is complete, they will notify the electronic resources coordinator, who will make sure that everything is in order, and then notify the appropriate personnel in the collection development department.

As can be seen, the electronic resources coordinator needs contact with all sides in order to make this process occur smoothly and in a timely fashion. While the process could occur with or without this coordinator's participation, the advantage of having a person in place in this position is that their specialized knowledge of the entire process, and their rapport with the IT and collection development departments helps to make it a smooth-flowing operation. With the ever-increasing demand for electronic products by library patrons, as well as a need to provide these products as quickly as possible, and also to ensure their continued upkeep and maintenance, it is becoming an ever-wiser investment for a library of a larger size to employ a librarian in this job.

Iowa State University's solution to bridging the CD-IT interface is certainly not the only one, but it does work well. Whatever an institution decides to do, they are going to have to, as Kaag says: " . . . talk to a number of people to determine the best process for your organization. It will undoubtedly be useful to find out what (if anything) has been done about handling online products in the past, talk to those who will be involved in the future, and draw up draft guidelines. . . ."[6] From these guidelines, a library can make educated determinations on how to tailor the best method of moving electronic products from the collection development department to the information technology department in that particular organization. As Kaag goes on to conclude: "It's especially important to make sure everyone understands that guidelines are not writ in stone, that change is inevitable and improvement is expected, and that the important thing is to get a process in place and adapt that process as experience teaches."[7] In other words, don't necessarily be married to a process for work between the two departments forever. If the process works, then immediate change may not be necessary, but in the fluid electronic environment, there will likely be a need for continuing revision of procedures dictating the work flow between the two areas, as well as from the always-educating process of experience, which will inevitably teach us which things work, and which don't.

CONCLUSIONS

A modern, technologically advanced academic library can no longer afford to maintain artificial barriers between different departments in its organizational chart, when those barriers will cost the library time and money, and hinder its advancement and growth in terms of resources, and as an institution. The electronic library is, by definition a seamless one, with users able to go from one resource to another with the click of a mouse, using the library only as the facilitating agency to enable this to happen. The library itself as a physical and organizational entity must strive to become more like its electronic offspring, and lower the barriers that keep its parts separated. The collection development department and the information technology department must work together more and more to help make this a reality. Mutual education and communication help to advance this process, and an electronic resources coordinator can help as well, serving as a mediating presence between the two camps in many instances.

NOTES

1. Cindy Stewart Kaag, "Collection Development for Online Serials: Who Needs to Do What, and Why, and When," *E-Serials: Publishers, Libraries, Users, and Standards*, ed. Wayne Jones (New York: The Haworth Press, Inc., 1998), p.119.

2. Cheryl LaGuardia and Stella Bentley, "Electronic Databases: Will Old Collection Development Policies Still Work?" *Online Magazine*, v. 16 (4), July 1992, p. 60.

3. Trisha L. Davis, "The Evolution of Selection Activities for Electronic Resources," *Library Trends*, v. 45 (3), Winter 1997, p. 391.

4. Arnold Hirshon, *Integrating Computing and Library Services (CAUSE Professional Paper Series #18)*, (Boulder, Colo.: CAUSE), p. 26.

5. David Fowler, Iowa State University Position Responsibility Statement for the position of Electronic Resources Coordinator, 1999.

6. Kaag, p. 110.

7. Ibid.

SPARC:
An Alternative Lifestyle
for Academic Libraries

Marina Oliver

INTRODUCTION

During the past twenty years publishers of scientific journals have held Academic Libraries captive. The Association of Research Libraries (ARL) reports that throughout the past decade the unit cost of a serial title has increased by 175% and ARL libraries have spent 124% more to purchase 7% fewer titles. At the same time, library budgets have decreased and the amount of published scientific information has increased exponentially. The results are serial cancellations, less book money, less funding for the Humanities and Social Sciences, resource sharing, and the formation of library consortial groups. However, the serial crisis has also led to the creation of the Scholarly Publishing and Academic Resources Coalition (SPARC). SPARC is a project of ARL and its member libraries; academic societies, university presses and other organizations that are interested in controlling the costs and improving the access to scholarly information. Libraries may finally have an alternative to high-priced scientific information.

OUR CURRENT SITUATION

Academic librarians are well aware of the current serial crisis. I say current, however, we've been in this predicament for almost 20 years.

[Haworth co-indexing entry note]: "SPARC: An Alternative Lifestyle for Academic Libraries." Oliver, Marina. Co-published simultaneously in *Collection Management* (The Haworth Information Press, an imprint of The Haworth Press, Inc.) Vol. 25, No. 1/2, 2000, pp. 37-49; and: *Electronic Collection Management* (ed: Suzan D. McGinnis) The Haworth Information Press, an imprint of The Haworth Press, Inc., 2000, pp. 37-49. Single or multiple copies of this article are available for a fee from The Haworth Document Delivery Service [1-800-342-9678, 9:00 a.m. - 5:00 p.m. (EST). E-mail address: getinfo@haworthpressinc.com].

37

The Association of Research Libraries (ARL) statistics shows that the unit cost per serial title has increased 175% since 1986. This sharp rise in subscription rates has led to one round of journal cancellations after another. Again ARL statistics provide a clear picture; they indicate that serial purchases have dropped by 7% between 1986 and 1998. During this same time period the median serial expenditures have risen 152% (Kyrillidou 1999). What this means for the academic community is that we're paying increasingly more for less information. Now factor into this already bleak scenario the growth in the amount of published research, the dominance of a few commercial publishers, exchange rate fluctuations, increase in the number of specialized journals being published and we find ourselves in a no-win situation. For additional proof, we merely need to look at the differences in the number of titles between the 1989 and 1997 editions of Ulrich's International Periodical Directory. Serial titles (in all academic disciplines) grew by 47% in less than ten years (Thomes, Clay 1998).

Libraries have tried a variety of strategies to alleviate this crisis: serial cancellations, document delivery, resource sharing, shifting funds from monographs to serials, all of which did little to improve an already austere situation. How did it get this far? Perhaps the following three profiles in the history of the serial crisis will help to explain the current situation.

Profile 1: Michael Rosenzweig and "Evolutionary Ecology"

Years ago, the publishing of scholarly communication was generally in the hands of university presses and professional/academic societies. Since these organizations are commonly not-for-profit institutions, subscription prices were relatively low. However, in the 1980s, commercial publishers found the Scientific, Technical and Medical (STM) market to be quite lucrative. A good example of this is the story of the journal *Evolutionary Ecology*. At a recent conference of the Association of College and Research Libraries, Michael Rosenzweig, Ph.D. Biologist and editor of SPARC's *Evolutionary Ecology Research*, shared his story. The following is a summary of Dr. Rosenzweig's account.

- 1984
  Michael Rosenzweig began work on a new journal for Chapman and Hall entitled *Evolutionary Ecology*. Subscription rate of $100/yr. for libraries and $35/yr. individuals

- 1987
  Chapman and Hall is a victim of a hostile takeover by International Thomson Corp. (ITC). ITC pays three times what others think Chapman and Hall is worth. (We all wonder why.)
- 1987-to-date
  Subscription rate for *Evolutionary Ecology* rises dramatically, cheaper binding is used, skilled employees leave and are eventually replaced by independent contractors, the publishing is decentralized and spread worldwide. For instance, the typesetters are in India, the printer is in Wales, and the mailing house is at ITC's international offices.
- 1998
  Evolutionary Ecology has 400 subscribers worldwide with an institutional subscription rate of $800/yr for a combination of print and on-line formats. Production and distribution costs are approximately $80,000/year. Total subscription income is between $250,000 and $300,000, a **275% markup**.

ITC is sold to Wolters Kluwer. Michael Rosenzweig and 90% of his authors leave *Evolutionary Ecology* and take their backlog of unpublished manuscripts with them. Kluwer believes they have the rights to the editorial board and the backlog of unpublished manuscripts. That is, they claimed more rights than they actually had. Lawyers get involved.

Rosenzweig, weary from his involvement with unscrupulous publishers, joins SPARC to begin a new journal entitled *Evolutionary Ecology Research*. The combination price for libraries is $305/yr. and any individual who belongs to a subscribing institution can have a print copy for $33/year. In addition, the journal authors own the copyright to their articles.

Profile II: Henry Barschall's 1988 Study of the Costs of Physics Journals

- 1988
  Henry Barschall, Professor of Physics at the University of Wisconsin Madison, conducted his second study of the costs of physics journals. Barschall found that the journals with the lowest cost per character ratios were those produced by scientific societies or associations. In contrast, he found that commercial pub-

lishers produced journals with high cost per character ratios. Barschall's report gave credence to what librarians already knew about the cost of scientific information. This study in itself was no great revelation to librarians; however, the effects the report had in the STM publishing community made Barschall's study a landmark event.

The Results:

Barschall's results were published in journals produced by the American Institute of Physics (AIP) and the American Physical Society (APS). The events that followed were astounding. AIP and APS used the study to promote their journals. Commercial publisher Gordon & Breach, whose journals were in the unflattering high cost to character category, sued AIP and APS claiming that Barschall's study was biased and represented "illegal comparative advertising" for the not-for-profit AIP and APS journals. The case went to U.S. District Court.

- 1997
  February–Henry Barschall dies just a few months short of the court's ruling.
  April–U.S. District Court rules in favor of AIP and APS stating ". . . defendants' physics journals as measured by cost per character and cost per character divided by impact factor are substantially more cost effective than those published by the plaintiffs." (ARL Bimonthly Report)

  A librarian could not have stated it better!

Profile III: Mark McCabe and the Portfolio Theory

- 1999
  Mark J. McCabe, Assistant Professor of Economics, Georgia Institute of Technology (GIT) publishes his study "Journal Pricing and Market Power." (Mark McCabe joined the GIT after seven years with the Department of Justice's Antitrust Division.) He approaches this study from the standpoint of antitrust analysis.

  Traditionally, according to McCabe, when analyzing a merger the Department of Justice (DOJ) determines the magnitude of the relevant market. That is, if the result of the merger would create a dominance by one company in the product market then the merger would be anticompetitive. Therefore the Department of Justice might require a divestiture or block the merger entirely.

However, the problem with mergers among academic publishers is that the markets are very narrowly defined. For example, from the DOJ's point of view, McCabe states, ". . . any journal is at best an imperfect substitute for any other journal . . . "; that is, there is little overlap in the product market. Consequently, the mergers appeared to be benign, so little antitrust action has been taken toward academic publishers.

With this in mind, McCabe conducts a study of STM journals and their publishers, which leads to the development of the "Portfolio Theory." One significant finding in the study was that given a set of similar titles, libraries do not necessarily subscribe to the journal with the best value. We tend to subscribe to groups of journals in broad subject areas and that cost per use is minimized across these areas. In other words, we are apt to purchase portfolios of journals rather than weigh one journal's value directly against another. Which is directly opposite the manner in which the academic publishing market has been defined by the DOJ.

The Portfolio Theory states, "Given libraries' demand for portfolios of titles within broad fields of study . . . all else equal, publishers set prices so that higher use (or quality) journals exhibit lower cost per use ratios. Thus, the higher-use journals are purchased by most libraries. Conversely, lower-use journals (that have higher cost per use) are purchased by fewer, relatively high-budget libraries."

Since libraries tend to purchase portfolios of titles, publishers have found that it is more profitable for them to sell high-use journals at lower costs to a wide customer base. They have also found that it is very profitable to sell lower-use journals at higher rates to fewer libraries even though they could sell them at much lower prices and still maintain a profit.

McCabe collected data on thousands of STM titles from 1988-1998. During this time, a number of large publishing mergers occurred, including Pergamon and Elsevier, and Lippincott and Kluwer. Concentrating on just the biomedical titles, McCabe found that each of these mergers was associated with significant price increases. For example, the Elsevier merger generated a 22% price increase for the former Pergamon titles and an 8% increase in Elsevier titles. According to McCabe, the data suggest that this price increase is due entirely to an increased share of the market.

The effect of the Kluwer merger was a 35% increase for former Lippincott titles. However, in this case, the price increase was due not only to an increased share of the market, but that Lippincott titles were now less likely to be cancelled by libraries.

McCabe concludes his study by saying ". . . cumulative evidence indicates that conventional antitrust procedures are inadequate for evaluating mergers in academic journal markets. First, market definition needs to be focused on broad portfolios of journal titles rather than a narrow content-based concept in order to reflect the reality of libraries' demand. Second, mergers involving relatively small companies can also have substantial price effects."

Although McCabe's research to-date is significant, he plans to continue this project by studying the impact of new titles on prices of established journals and comparing the difference in behavior between for-profit and not-for-profit publishers. It will be interesting to read McCabe's updates as this study continues, especially with the addition of a new player, ARL's Scholarly Publishing and Academic Resources Coalition (SPARC).

It is clear from these profiles why the costs of STM journals have risen to a crisis level. However, libraries no longer need to be victims of high journal prices. We now have an alternative.

THE ALTERNATIVE

The Scholarly Publishing and Academic Resource Coalition (SPARC) began to take shape in Spring 1998. That is when the Association of American Universities (AAU), the Association of American University Presses (AAUP), and the Big 12 Chief Academic Officers all gave their support to the American Association of Research Libraries (ARL) to launch an alternative to the current system of scholarly communication. SPARC is an effort by ARL, its member libraries, academic societies, university presses and other organizations to control the costs and improve the access to scholarly information. SPARC's mission is to "be a mechanism for change in academic publishing by creating a more economical marketplace for research information, encourage innovative uses of technology to improve scholarly communication and advance the academic principles of access to information for research and teaching."

Toward this mission, SPARC and its partners advocate the following values:

- The fostering of a competitive market for scholarly publishing by encouraging new publishers that are committed to the principles of cost-based pricing,
- The implementation of policies for intellectual property management emphasizing the ethical use of scholarly resources,
- The innovative applications of technology to expand research, scholarship and distribution of information,
- The assurance that these new channels of scholarly communication maintains quality requirements and contribute to the promotion and tenure process, and
- To enable the permanent archiving of research publications in traditional and electronic formats.

Having high values and innovative ideas is not enough to make the SPARC initiative successful. What is it about this endeavor that makes it so promising? ARL suggests the following:

- SPARC has qualified, skilled partners ready to work with research institutions to open new avenues for scholarly publishing.
- Librarians are fed up with rising journal costs and are now prepared to financially support new forms of scholarly publishing.
- The internet has made it possible for research to be published quickly by just about anyone.
- University administrators are now prepared to support new forms of scholarly publishing.

In short, the academic community has grown impatient with many of the STM for-profit publishers; the technology is readily available, the authors are eager and the price is right.

SPARC began with the financial support of 81 ARL member libraries, all of which also agreed to subscribe to all SPARC products. According to ARL these libraries have a combined purchasing power of approximately 500 million dollars. This means that SPARC publishing partners have an instant subscriber base, a virtually no-lose situation for the publisher. The converse is also true, that is, SPARC's publishing partners are committed to controlling product costs and willing to launch quality publications in subject areas (STM) which are dominated by higher-priced commercial titles. Therefore, SPARC member libraries are in a no-lose situation.

As of October 1999, SPARC library membership has grown to 175 members, 144 full members, 21 consortial members and 10 supporting members. Full membership requires an annual contribution of $7500 and a commitment to purchase the current SPARC titles. Consortial members commit to purchase 0.2% of their materials budget and supporting members have no purchase commitment.

In June 1998, SPARC announced its first publishing partner, the prestigious American Chemical Society (ACS). ACS' first journal, *Organic Letters*, began in July 1999 and is available in both print and electronic formats. A refereed journal, *Organic Letters* boasts an editorial team that includes 3 Nobel Prize laureates. The subscription cost for *Organic Letters* is one quarter the price of its competitor. What is so convincing, as Rick Johnson SPARC Enterprise Director points out, is that with the money saved libraries could purchase all of the following titles:

- *Chemical Communications*
- *Physical Chemistry Chemical Physics*
- *New Journal of Chemistry*
- *Methods in Organic Synthesis*
- *Natural Product Updates*
- *Dalton Transactions*
- *Journal of Materials Chemistry*
- *Journal of Chemical Research*
- *Natural Product Reports*
- *Chemical Society Reviews*
- *Annual Reports on the Progress of Chemistry: Parts A, B and C*
- *Journal of Green Chemistry*
- *Faraday Discussions*
- *The Analyst*
- *Analytical Communications*
- *Journal of Analytical Atomic Spectrometry*
- *Journal of Environmental Monitoring*

ACS has committed to add one title per year for the next three years. Their second journal, *Crystal Growth & Design,* is now available.

Another impressive publishing partner is the Royal Society of Chemistry (RSC). RSC also has committed to produce three journals over the next three years. Their first journal, *PhysChemComm,* is refereed and available in electronic format only.

Michael Rosenzweig's *Evolutionary Ecology Research* (EER) began in January 1999 at an institutional subscription rate of just $290 for print format and $305 for a combination of paper and electronic access. The combined price is just over one-third the subscription rate of Wolters-Kluwer's publication, *Evolutionary Ecology.* In addition, individuals affiliated with each subscribing institution can obtain personal copies for $33/year in the U.S. and $41 elsewhere.

SPARC currently directs three programs: the Alternatives Program, Leading Edge Program and the Scientific Communities Initiative. The Alternative Program supports publications that have the potential to be in direct competition with existing higher-priced STM journals. SPARC requires that the new product must offer member libraries a quality journal at a lower price. Hopefully, this will allow libraries to reduce the number of high-priced STM journals they currently subscribe to and redirect their materials budget to other subject areas.

It should be noted that according to SPARC they are not a journals publisher or distributor, and has no financial interest in partnered projects. Their role is to enable and support projects that contribute to a more competitive marketplace (SPARC Feb. 1998).

The American Chemical Society, Royal Society of Chemistry and Evolutionary Ecology Research are members of the Alternatives Program. Potential partners for all three programs are chosen based on the basis of a set of selection criteria. In general, the proposed product must be marketable and the content and quality should rival existing higher priced journals. The project should be financially viable and a potential partner should have a reputation, which is compatible with SPARC's values and goals. A detailed list of selection criteria can be found at *www.arl.org/sparc/alt.html.*

SPARC describes the Leading Edge Program as an initiative which "supports ventures that contribute to a shift in technology use, introduce or demonstrate innovative business models and/or address the information needs of an emerging or fast growing STM field"

(SPARC Jan. 1998). The essence of the Leading Edge program is for researchers to have a reliable outlet in which to publish their information and in turn their colleagues have a reputable resource in which to access this information. More information on the Leading Edge program can be found at *www.arl.org/sparc/edge.html.*

As part of the Leading Edge Program, the distinguished Institute of Physics and Germany Physical Society are currently producing the peer reviewed electronic journal "New Journal of Physics." Also, an independent group of chemists in the U.S., U.K., and Germany, are producing the electronic "Internet Journal of Chemistry" (IJC). What makes IJC so unique, editor Steve Bachrach points out, is that "authors can publish the full 3-D structures of molecules, use color images free of charge, represent dynamic processes in a movie or animation, publish large data sets, and allow readers to manipulate spectra" (SPARC Oct. 1999).

SPARC's Scientific Communities Initiative (SCI) is designed to support non-profit digital projects that will change the scientific scholarly communication market. By financially supporting theses ventures SPARC hopes to foster the creation of new information communities to better serve the science/technology researcher. The expectation is that these communities will have their origins in partnerships within universities and professional societies. In 1999 SPARC's SCI program awarded approximately $500,000 in grant money to such digital projects as Columbia University Press's Columbia Earthscape, the California Digital Library's eScholarship, and MIT's CogNet.

Columbia Earthscape is multimedia resource that covers subject areas such as oceanography, geology, climatic studies and environmental resources. It currently consists of full-text books, video clips, journal articles, lectures, seminars, policy papers, maps, searchable databases and live webcasts from such notable organizations as Columbia, NASA, MIT, the American Museum of Natural History and ABC News (Columbia 1999). It is designed as a resource not only for researchers but also for all of us who are interested in the environment.

The California Digital Library's eScholarship "will support scholar-led innovations in scholarly communication by providing an infrastructure for experimentation. The first part includes an electronic print (e-print) database system; the second part includes a set of support services and community building activities for its use. Initially, eScholarship will focus on creating electronic publications and support services that build upon and extend existing, proven innovations in this area. Planned objectives include: development and deployment of the eScholarship Archive, initially by mirroring and extending the Los Alamos National Laboratory *xxx* e-print server; creation of new and linkage of existing digital journals; implementation and support services for community-led innovations; and integration of digital publishing and digital access" (Buckholtz 1999).

The third initiative, MIT CogNet is an electronic community for the cognitive and brain sciences. CogNet includes a library of full-text books, journals and reference works; job listings, editorials, threaded discussions, virtual poster sessions, almanac of academic cognitive science programs and much more. Additional information can be obtained at <*http://cognet.mit.edu/welcome.html*>.

Separate from SCI is a new digital initiative, BioOne, which involves SPARC, academe, commercial publishers and scientific societies. BioOne is a non-profit project made possible through the collaboration of the following organizations: SPARC, American institute of Biological Sciences (AIBS), the Big 12 Plus Libraries Consortium, University of Kansas and Allen Press. The website will consist of journals and bulletins produced by AIBS's 55 member societies. Users will be able to perform cross-journal searches and inter-journal linking from references. Beta testing is scheduled for early 2001 and will be available to the public (by subscription) shortly thereafter (SPARC Oct. 1999).

CONCLUSION

For years, the academic community has been at the mercy of unscrupulous journal publishers. Journal prices soared as our budgets were cut or remained stagnant. We cancelled serials, shifted funds and became active proponents for resource sharing, none of which was a concern or made an impact on the publishing community. Finally, an organization exists that offers an alternative to high-priced STM publishers, the Scholarly Publishing and Academic Resources Coalition. SPARC's commitment to high-quality, low-cost access to scientific information along with the financial support from member libraries and the commitment of such distinguished publishing partners as the Royal Society of Chemistry, Institute of Physics and the American Chemical Society, will make SPARC a significant force in the scientific publishing community. We now have an alternative to high-priced STM journals. It is our responsibility to support this venture and show the commercial publishers that we will not and do not have to pay their prices any longer.

NOTES

Buckholtz, Alison, "SPARC's Scientific Communities Initiative Awards Grants Worth A Half-million Dollars" *Association of Research Libraries Page* (Oct. 1999) *http://www.arl.org/sparc/grants.html*

Byrd, Gary D., "An Economic "Commons" Tragedy for Research Libraries: Scholarly Journal Publishing and Pricing Trends," *College & Research Libraries* 51:184-95 (May 1990).

Johnson, Rick, "SPARC: Sparking Competition in the Scholarly Publishing Marketplace," *Association of Research Libraries Page* (1999) http://www.arl.org/sparc/ppt/

Johnson, Richard K., "SPARC Whitepaper," *Association of Research Libraries Page* (April 1999) *http://www.arl.org/sparc/whitepaper.html*

Kyrillidou, Martha, "Spending More for Less . . .," *ARL Bimonthly Report* 204 (June 1999) *http://www.arl.org/newsltr/204/spending.html*

Marshall, Lauren, "Another Innovative On-line, Multi-media Resource–Columbia Earthscape–Launched by Columbia," *Columbia University Page* (Nov. 1999) *http://www.columbia.edu/cu/news/archive/99/11/earthscape.html*

McCabe, Mark J. "The Impact of Publisher Mergers on Journal Prices: An Update," *ARL Bimonthly Report* 207 (Dec. 1999). *http://www.arl.org/newsltr/207/jrnlprices.html*

MIT CogNet, "The Cognitive and Brain Sciences Community Online," *CogNet Page, http://cognet.mit.edu/welcome.html*

Powell, Allen, "Serials Pricing–An Agent's View: Trends and Characteristics of Higher Education Funding and STM Journal Pricing," *The Serials Librarian* 36(1-2):253-262 (1999).

Rosenzweig, Michael L., "Reclaiming What We Own: Expanding Competition in Scholarly Publishing," *Association of Research Libraries Page* (April 1999) *http://www.arl.org/sparc/rosenzweig.html*

Soete, George and Athena Salabe "The Barschall Legacy" in "Measuring the Cost Effectiveness of Journals: the Wisconsin Experience," *Bimonthly Report* 205 (Sept. 1999). *http://www.arl.org/newsltr/205/wisconsin.html*.

SPARC, "SPARC Alternatives Program," *Association of Research Libraries Page* (Feb. 1998) *http://www.arl.org/sparc/alt.html*

SPARC, "Announcing: the SPARC Scientific Communities Initiative," *Association of Research Libraries Page* (May 1999) *http://www.arl.org/sparc/sci.html*

SPARC, "Introducing a Response to Soaring Journal Prices: SPARC An Initiative of the Association of Research Libraries," *Association of Research Libraries Page* (Nov. 1999) *http://www.arl.org/sparc/factsheet.html*

SPARC, "Introduction to the Publisher Partnership Program," *Association of Research Libraries Page* (Feb. 1998) *http://www.arl.org/sparc/intro.html*

SPARC, "Public-Private Collaboration Develops BioOne, Providing Online, Full-Text Access to Aggregated Database of Bioscience Research Journals," *Association of Research Libraries Page* (Oct. 1999)

SPARC, "SPARC Leading Edge Program," *Association of Research Libraries Page* (Jan. 1998) *http://www.arl.org/sparc/edge.html*

Stoller, Michael A., Christopherson, Robert and Michael Miranda, "The Economics of Professional Journal Pricing," *College & Research Libraries* 57:9-21 (Jan. 1996).

Thompson, James C., "Journal Costs: Perception and Reality in the Dialogue," *College & Research Libraries* 49(6):481-482 (Nov. 1988).

Challenges in Electronic Collection Building in Interdisciplinary Studies

Kristin H. Gerhard

INTRODUCTION

There is no question that the full-scale explosion of electronic information sources has complicated the work of collection development librarians. Significant impacts include impacts on materials budgets, patron expectations, libraries technological needs and the knowledge and abilities needed by librarians to perform their jobs effectively in a new kind of library. Both the art and science necessary to perform high quality collection development work have changed because of the impact of new electronic formats being used for delivery of information.

The work of subject specialist librarians with collections responsibilities for interdisciplinary areas has been similarly impacted by the increasing emphasis on electronic resources in library collections. But interdisciplinary subject areas present their own unique difficulties to the collections librarian. Adding electronic information products to the mix increases the complexities of collecting materials that support interdisciplinary scholarship, and can have a disparate affect on the work of collections librarians in these areas. The situation is more complicated for librarians working in interdisciplinary subject areas: how can they identify which impacts are simply challenges because of the shift towards remote access/electronic products, and which im-

[Haworth co-indexing entry note]: "Challenges in Electronic Collection Building in Interdisciplinary Studies." Gerhard, Kristin H. Co-published simultaneously in *Collection Management* (The Haworth Information Press, an imprint of The Haworth Press, Inc.) Vol. 25, No. 1/2, 2000, pp. 51-65; and: *Electronic Collection Management* (ed: Suzan D. McGinnis) The Haworth Information Press, an imprint of The Haworth Press, Inc., 2000, pp. 51-65. Single or multiple copies of this article are available for a fee from The Haworth Document Delivery Service [1-800-342-9678, 9:00 a.m. - 5:00 p.m. (EST). E-mail address: getinfo@haworthpressinc.com].

51

pacts are disparately affecting interdisciplinary areas, so that they can respond appropriately to the challenges before them?

DEFINITION OF INTERDISCIPLINARY

The academic landscape is increasingly interdisciplinary. Klein gives a detailed description of the evolution of academic disciplines and interdisciplinary in her seminal work *Interdisciplinary: History, Theory, & Practice.* Her discussion of the available understandings of interdisciplinary suggests four typical approaches to defining it:

Interdisciplinary is usually defined in one of four ways:
1. *by example,* to designate what form it assumes;
2. *by motivation,* to explain why it takes place;
3. *by principles of interaction,* to demonstrate the process of how disciplines interact; and
4. *by terminological hierarchy,* to distinguish levels of integration by using specific labels.[1]

Much of the debate on the definition of interdisciplinary has focused on the fourth of these possibilities, leading to discussions of multidisciplinary, cross-disciplinarily, and so forth. In Klein's seminal work on interdisciplinary, she uses the terms interdisciplinary and integrative interchangeably.[2] Her focus is on the ways that knowledge is generated by integrating the concepts, instruments, and developments of more than one discipline. She notes that all interdisciplinary activities are rooted in the ideas of unity and synthesis, evoking a common epistemology of convergence.[3]

Ryan, in his discussion of the role of the collection development librarian in an increasingly interdisciplinary world, suggests that this world does not so much generate new areas of specialization as it blurs and melds older ones. In promoting relationships among fields, it challenges the viability of investing too heavily in specialization and narrow forms of expertise. It privileges and rewards discourses among fields rather than conversations within them. It values synthetic as opposed to merely technical skills. It defines excellence more in terms of ability to make connections across the field of play than the persistence needed to excavate a deep hole.[4]

Academic librarians have long been aware of the shifting and evolving nature of the universities whose needs they serve. We know which departments and programs are firmly established, which are just getting off the ground. Departments and programs are added as well as eliminated due to changes in institutional focus or market forces; as an example, Iowa State University has seen the elimination of a major in Leisure Studies and the addition of a major in Women's Studies over the past decade. The AAUP is currently studying the academic publishing output published over the past ten years "to establish whether some academic specialties should be listed as endangered species."[5]

Hur-Li Lee points out that the historically well-established disciplines have received more consistent support from academic libraries and the librarians responsible for building local collections. She continues,

> By contrast, newer disciplines and interdisciplinary fields of study can suffer tremendously from a lack of cooperation and adequate funding in collection development . . . librarians endorse traditional disciplinary structures by prolonging the disciplinary approach in their work. If the clientele served by the library is becoming less discipline-bound while the library remains disciplinary, how can objectivity be claimed in collections decisions?[6]

The advent of widespread electronic resources, and the concomitant electronic libraries they make possible, provide a clear opportunity for collection development librarians to redress this historical imbalance.

THE RISE OF ELECTRONIC RESOURCES IN LIBRARIES

The advent and subsequent explosion of electronic information sources in libraries has received wide attention in the library science community. Books, articles, and conference programs on this subject abound to the point where it seems almost trite to underline the fundamental nature of the changes our collections are undergoing as a result. Coutts provides a good summary of our current situation and its opportunities:

> The latest development to be assimilated by research libraries is the electronic environment. As it has developed, it has become

clear that the exceptional power and potential of the new medium will force fundamental changes in research collections. These will be evident in the nature of the collections and services, which are, developed by individual libraries or information services, and in the role that resource sharing will play in the future. As electronic provision becomes part of core collections and services, it is timely to consider the ways in which the practicing research library is adjusting in order to smooth the researcher's work, and the more distant changes for which it must prepare now.[7]

Among the specific issues she identifies are questions about comprehensiveness of local collections, and the impact of this comprehensiveness (or its lack) on the researcher; cooperative collection development; and the increase in volume and cost of information as more becomes available in the electronic format.

New methods of disseminating information for research are multiplying and include electronic discussion lists, conferences, bulletin boards, and Usenet and its newsgroups. Most powerful and revolutionary of all, multimedia is allowing text to be combined with still or moving images, sound and three-dimensional representations of artifacts in a world of virtual reality, where the user may be able to interact or participate with the publication.[8]

Among the issues raised for libraries in this new environment are the unwillingness of some patrons to use print sources, issues of copyright and control of the scholarly communication system, and the ways in which electronic resources may be integrated into universities' distance education programs–or may be overlooked entirely as distance education programs are planned.

In an editorial, Martello suggests that, when it comes to electronic information resources, "The challenge we face is to determine how much of this information relates directly to the academic curriculum."[9] He predicts a 1-5% conversion of print resources to electronic format over next 10 years. He notes further that "looking ahead 10 years to predict what percentage of collection development funds will be spent on non-bibliographic electronic resources is more perplexing."[10] There are many planning issues to be dealt with as we move into an increasingly electronic future. Where will our management data come from? What information do we need in order to make the best collections-related decisions possible in the face of an unclear future?

INFORMATION NEEDS
OF INTERDISCIPLINARY SCHOLARS

Lynn Westbrook's study of interdisciplinary information seeking behavior of women's studies faculty discusses both the anticipated needs of interdisciplinary scholars (based on the literature) as well as fairly comprehensive findings about the actual information seeking behavior of this group. Researchers in interdisciplinary subjects face difficulties in finding relevant documents, scattered information sources, lack of appropriate databases or other reference sources for their area, and the need for librarian support and direction in negotiating this terrain.[11] In practice, Westbrook found that these researchers place a high value on browsing, the knowledge of colleagues, making connections among ideas, using computers, tapping into a full range of information resources (including people), and related their teaching and research to one another.[12]

The reliance on browsing and human interaction is also discussed by Olsen in her book on electronic journal literature:

The first problem is that the selection of literature, which is optimal for an individual, requires human, not computer recognition. The particular requirements identified by scholars to overcome this problem are as follows: . . . Experiencing serendipity to locate an article which would not have been found otherwise, and to make chance visual connections with an author's phrase or sentence which unpredictably stimulates a new line of thought; searching in a non-predetermined manner to gather "outlier" articles on a topic and to generate new ideas; browsing to support ongoing education where the boundaries of what is "appropriate" literature are not, and should not be, fixed; and participation visually with a wide body of literature.[13]

The literature used by scholars doing research or teaching in interdisciplinary areas is broader than that used by scholars in traditional disciplines. Interdisciplinary researchers are likely to rely on both the research published in their home discipline, and on work being published in other established disciplines. In addition, these scholars may be using explicitly interdisciplinary resources when they are available.

A straightforward explanation for Westbrook's findings on the difficulties of finding relevant documents among the information scatter is given by Lee. She suggests that one explanation for the more laborious information seeking in interdisciplinary research is the inflexible, long-lived disciplinary structures underlying information organization. University libraries, like universities, are organized by discipline ... Once the disciplinary structures are in place, new fields that do not fit in will have to be handled as special cases."[14]

These ideas are further supported by a cross-disciplinary survey of faculty and graduate student library use conducted by Maughan. The goal of the project was to collect management information that could be used in developing or improving information systems and services.[15] Her research sample included faculty and graduate students in Latin American studies, an interdisciplinary field.

A comparatively high percentage (57%) of Latin American studies faculty reported browsing sometimes or often, while 80% search print indexes and bibliographies sometimes or often.[16] This interdisciplinary programs faculty also had the highest percentage of asking a librarian for advice on finding research materials. The Latin American studies group also had the highest attendance at library research workshops. Latin American studies respondents had more experience with document delivery services such as interlibrary loan than their peers:

> There was very little familiarity among those surveyed with the library-provided document delivery service. With the exception of Latin American studies, the majority of respondents, ranging from 80% (ancient history and Mediterranean archeology) to 94% (classics), reported insufficient experiences with the document delivery service to evaluate it.[17]

In her discussion, Maughan points out that subjects in the social sciences and area studies appeared to be far more likely to seek the advice of librarians in addressing their information needs (either by relying on instructional or reference services provided by the library) than were their peers in other fields. She asks, why is this? Is it because their information resources are more diffuse than other disciplines, more extensive or interdisciplinary, more difficult to identify, that more of them are in electronic form, or in several different formats concurrently?[18]

She also notes that these respondents also had the highest response to the need for information published on a daily basis, and suggests that these researchers might benefit from the development of SCI services.

Coutts summarizes this point nicely, saying that "Electronic information represents an outstanding opportunity to meet the known needs of the research community and to stimulate new lines of exploration and work methods to pursue them."[19] This is especially true for interdisciplinary research and teaching efforts.

KNOWLEDGE DISCOVERY

The challenge of identifying relevant information resources for specific interdisciplinary research enterprises, both for the librarian and for the scholar, is not a minor one. There is considerably more information available today than ever before, and the interdisciplinary researcher must be able to look broadly for the information that will meet her or his needs. There is a need for information filters that can be set widely enough open to allow serendipitous discovery.

In the absence of well-developed SCI services, how does the researcher identify the relevant resources for the project in hand? Sources must be identified or discovered in some way. According to Branin, librarians need to be knowledge managers, not collection managers, in our new electronic world.[20]

This is one of the places where technological advance paired with traditional library practice has the potential to serve our users well. The development of metadata and other approaches to cataloging electronic information sources provides interdisciplinary users with a wide range of tools that can aid in the quest for relevant information. Coutts suggests that "the combination of catalogues, indexes, gateways and search engines forms the basis of the new 'bibliographic control' to meet the researcher's information needs. As our experience of it develops in tandem with the technology, it will change and be refined to become an ever more sophisticated means of resource discovery."[21]

AVAILABILITY AND DEVELOPMENT OF ELECTRONIC RESOURCES FOR INTERDISCIPLINARY AREAS

The increase in availability of electronic products over the past decade has resulted in some interdisciplinary products being developed. As noted above, however, these interdisciplinary products have tended to lag behind development of electronic resources for more established disciplines. Where chemistry and economics have relatively well-developed and well-established electronic resources appropriate to the needs of researchers in those fields, it has only been in recent years that a field such as women's studies had so much as an electronic citational database. The shift from no electronic titles, to indexing and abstracting services, to full-text has come more slowly for interdisciplinary areas. There are critical roles for subject specialists to play in encouraging vendors to develop appropriate resources for these areas, and there are frequently opportunities for subject specialists to contribute to the creation of these resources.

In assessing potential electronic purchases, it is important to remember that interdisciplinary researchers do rely on disciplinary sources as well as what interdisciplinary materials they are able to identify. It is therefore important to have a good grasp of the degree of coverage of the interdisciplinary area in question by traditional indexing sources and tables of contents services.[22]

A final trend in the availability of electronic titles that affects interdisciplinary areas disparately is the trend towards vendors and publishers offering electronic titles as packages or bundles. Explicitly interdisciplinary resources may not be included in groups created by vendor, particularly if they are offering packages organized around the historical/established disciplines. This is another area where advocacy and action on the part of librarians is needed if we are to meet the needs of integrative scholarship.

COLLECTION EVALUATION
FOR INTERDISCIPLINARY MATERIALS

The rapid increase in electronic titles has in some cases (for more established interdisciplinary areas) resulted in the sudden availability of multiple sources, an embarrassment of riches from which librarians must find a way to select. Among methods useful in this situation are trial periods, evaluation by key faculty as well as by librarians, the establishment of criteria for comparison, and comments from librarians at other institutions. An example of a study comparing new electronic resources in an interdisciplinary area is Dickstein et al.'s examination of four new women's studies electronic titles.[23]

Evaluating electronic resources is challenging enough, given the widely ranging availability and quality of usage statistics for these products. Most of the traditional evaluation techniques can be applied to electronic resources as well as they have been to print titles. Assessment of interdisciplinary electronic sources does present some unique challenges. How does the librarian identify which faculty are the appropriate ones from whom to get feedback? How does the library go about defining the potential user pool for an interdisciplinary product? For that matter, how does the library take into consideration use of disciplinary resources by interdisciplinary researchers from a different home discipline? These questions have particular significance for publicity strategies and assessing the impact of publicity on usage when a title is being evaluated for an ongoing subscription.

Dobson et al. provides a comprehensive approach to collection evaluation for interdisciplinary areas, which includes an assessment of technological support and document delivery services.[24] In keeping with this approach, Coutts notes the need for established standards of service support, suggesting that, for electronic resources, more support rather than less is probably needed.[25] Johnson also notes that selecting traditional resources has not often required the selector to consider the skills the users will need, how they will be taught, and who will teach them."[26] Given the greater reliance that interdisciplinary scholars place on librarians, this has particular significance for librarians planning collections and services to support interdisciplinary subjects.

COOPERATIVE COLLECTION DEVELOPMENT

The high cost of, and complications of licensing, electronic resources has resulted in the formation of many library consortia. The intent is to increase purchasing power of individual libraries by making purchases as a group. This approach can also simplify the licensing process, where licensing standards are held in common by the consortial members. For interdisciplinary topics, consortial purchasing can represent a challenge. Initially, consortia tend to focus on general or well established, basic resources. As consortia grow in experience and buying power, attention must be paid to whether interdisciplinary titles are included in consortial purchasing agreements, or whether they are seen as too marginal or secondary to be included in consortial planning.

The other face of cooperative collection development is resource sharing. As Coutts notes, "An inevitable product of effective resource discovery is the researcher's desire to access information not available as part of his or her local collection."[27] For interdisciplinary scholars, the ability to obtain a wide range of material in a timely way can be particularly important. Technological advances coupled with burgeoning electronic titles are allowing libraries the opportunity to increase the speed of document delivery.

BUDGET STREAMS
FOR INTERDISCIPLINARY COLLECTION SUPPORT

Budgeting for interdisciplinary areas has always had inherent difficulty. Depending on institutional history and need, any interdisciplinary subject could be budgeted completely separately with its own budget line, given no budget at all (with the assumption that these materials will be picked up by budget lines assigned to well-established disciplines as the materials are needed), or some middle point between these extremes. Some interdisciplinary resources may be purchased cooperatively by a group of bibliographers, each contributing some proportion of the total cost. Any of these scenarios can leave interdisciplinary materials falling between the gaps of assigned budget lines.

This situation is intensified in libraries where the materials and access budget is already squeezed by the need to maintain the physical collections while building the electronic library. If an important interdisciplinary electronic resource overlaps to any degree with traditional disciplinary resources, it can be politically difficult to fund the interdisciplinary title. The problem is only more clear when an interdisciplinary product has significant cumulative overlaps across multiple disciplinary products.

These difficulties can be overcome to some extent by consistent and persistent communication among bibliographers. There is also a need for strong support for important interdisciplinary programs from library administrators responsible for the collections area. In libraries with an electronic resources committee making recommendations for purchase, it is important that committee members have appropriate education in the nature of interdisciplinary research.

EDUCATION AND TRAINING
FOR INTERDISCIPLINARY COLLECTION DEVELOPMENT

The increasingly interdisciplinary nature of academic research alone has important implications for the preparation of subject specialist librarians who will take on collection development responsibilities. Add to this shift the movement towards the electronic library and there are a number of areas where education and training for collection development could be strengthened. The keys are education and integration.

The electronic environment allows for more merging and melding of disciplines and widens the array of materials that can be drawn on by any one researcher. This contrasts with more traditional, hierarchically organized print sources. The World Wide Web, for example, is connective and integrative rather than hierarchical. An understanding of the potential of electronic resources, and of the nature of disciplinary and interdisciplinary knowledge, are both important to the academic collection development librarian in today's environment.

Lee found that librarians she studied did not have a strong understanding of interdisciplinary or interdisciplinary work. She says, "In general, interdisciplinary work to librarians means any intellectual activity that involves more than one field, or discipline, regardless how or what the fields contribute to the work."[28] It is important for subject specialists to understand the wide range of possibilities covered by the term interdisciplinary, and to be able to describe more precisely the ways in which the fields they work with could be defined to be interdisciplinary.

Ackerson conducted a study to visualize the configuration of disciplinary relationships in basic scientific literature. She believes that having a conceptual model of how information is disseminated and organized, along with a better understanding of disciplinary relationships, enables researchers to plan more effective strategies for gathering information.[29] Based on her data analysis, Ackerson posits a view of scientific literature as multidimensional, with a honeycombed, web-like structure of internal relationships. She states that if scientific literature is envisioned as multidimensional (i.e., as a mosaic or honeycomb), there is a tendency to search not only in the primary discipline but to spread the search for information across related disciplines as well to achieve a more complete search.[30] This is the kind of understanding that collection development librarians need to come to in the course of their education and training.

As discussed above, librarians can play a significant role as advocates for development of needed, appropriate products. They can also advocate for development of products by learned societies, rational pricing and licensing, for appropriate, state-of-the-art user interfaces, and so forth. There is a particular need, however, for librarians who advocate effectively for both technical and content developments that will serve a growing range of interdisciplinary scholars. Interfaces that allow simple and unified searching of multiple, interrelated databases, for example, could be particularly useful in integrative research.

Training in appropriate technologies needs to be extended to all collection development librarians. Selection of electronic resources requires that the selector understand the hardware and software needs involved, and be able to assess the best level of platform for the particular product. For some interdisciplinary products, the audience will be small and a single-station CD-ROM access within the library building may suffice. For others, the audience may be quite large, crossing many disciplines, and a site license may make sense. Without understanding what equipment and expertise is available to provide local access to a resource, there is no way to come to rational collection decisions.

Gorman points out that, "from the librarian's and, most important, the library user's point of view, the 'collection' is that universe of materials that is readily and freely available."[31] As libraries are challenged to identify how much access is needed, and how best to pay for this access to the collection broadly conceived, collection development librarians will need to conceive of their work in equally broad terms. Coutts suggests that "As the experience of researchers and information specialists grows, there will be many new and variant services devised to meet the user's needs. The exploration of the possibilities should become one of the most challenging and stimulating of the information specialist's duties."[32] For librarians working with interdisciplinary subject matter, this statement is particularly apt. Whether working on a product proposal, product development, recommendations to strengthen an existing product, or potential approaches to strategic dissemination of information in a given area, there is a plethora of interesting and useful projects for the energetic collections librarian.

CONCLUSION

Buckland, writing on what collection developers will do in the future suggests that, up until recently, each user of any one library was supplied with the same collection. He points to the high regard with which faculty hole their branch libraries as coming from their being customized to special needs as well as from their geographical convenience.[33] He proposes viewing the electronic library of the future as serving topical rather than geographical communities. Because new technology is significantly more flexible than that of paper and cardboard, making multiple alternative approaches more feasible, issues of value and privileging now need to be addressed in more complex ways. Fundamentally, this involves a shift from traditional standardized provision in one or a few ways towards more flexible systems, designed to be adaptive and more responsive to users desires to invoke their own preferences in exploring the universe of documents.[34]

Customization of information for interdisciplinary researchers will require collection development librarians to develop and exercise new skills. They will need to have a strong grasp of the interdisciplinary enterprise, of the potential of information technologies as they develop, and the subject resources available for the research area at hand. Only with these abilities in place will collections librarians be able to meet the needs of interdisciplinary scholars.

NOTES

1.Klein, Julie Thompson. *Interdisciplinary: History, Theory, & Practice.* Detroit: Wayne State University Press, 1990, p. 55.

2. I. Klein, p. 15.

3. II. Klein, p. 11.

4. Ryan, Michael T. Among the Disciplines: The Bibliographer in the I World. In: Peggy Johnson and Sheila S. Intner, eds., *Recruiting, Educating, and Training Librarians for Collection Development.* Westport, CT: Greenwood Press, 1994 *(New Directions in Information Management*, No. 3), p. 106.

5. Ruark, Jennifer K. University Presses to Examine Whether Some Fields Are in Danger of Disappearing. *Chronicle of Higher Education* (http://chronicle.com), September 22, 1999.

6. Lee, Hur-Li. *Toward a Reconceptualization of Collection Development: A Study of the Collecting of Women's Studies Materials by a University Library System.* New Brunswick, NJ: Rutgers, The State University of New Jersey, 1997 (Dissertation), p. 43.

7. Coutts, Margaret M. Collecting for the Researcher in an Electronic Environment, *Library Review*, v. 47 no. 5/6, p. 282-283.

8. Coutts, p. 283.

9. Martello, Charles. Editorial: Not by a Long Shot and Other Wagers, *Journal of Academic Librarianship*, v. 21 (Jan. 1995), p. 1.

10. Martello, p. 2.

11. Westbrook, Lynn. *Interdisciplinary Information Seeking in Women's Studies.* Jefferson, NC: McFarland, 1999, p. 25-46.

12. Westbrook, p. 109-130.

13. Olsen, Jan. Electronic Journal Literature: Implications for Scholars. Westport, CT: Mecklermedia, 1994, p. 63.

14. Lee, p. 156-7.

15. Maughan, Patricia Davitt. A Library Resources and Services: A Cross-Disciplinary Survey of Faculty and Graduate Student Use and Satisfaction. *Journal of Academic Librarianship*, v. 25 (Sept. 1999), p. 355.

16. Maughan, p. 368.

17. Maughan, p. 360.

18. Maughan, p. 364.

19. Coutts, p. 283.

20. Branin, Joseph J. Fighting Back Once Again: From Collection Management to Knowledge Management. In: Peggy Johnson and Bonnie MacEwan, eds., *Collection Management and Development: Issues in an Electronic Era: Proceedings of the Advanced Collection Management and Development Institute, Chicago, Illinois, March 26-28, 1993.* Chicago: American Library Association, 1994 (*ALCTS Papers on Library Technical Services and Collections*, no. 5), p. xiv.

21. Coutts, p. 285.

22. See, for example, Kristin H. Gerhard, Trudi Jacobson and Susan G. Williamson, Indexing Adequacy and Interdisciplinary Journals: the Case of Women's Studies. *College and Research Libraries* v. 54 (March 1993), pp. 125-35; Cindy Faries, Preserving the Value of Tables of Contents Online: A Critique of Women's Studies/Feminist Periodicals. In: Kristin H. Gerhard, ed. *Women's Studies Serials: A Quarter-Century of Development.* New York: Haworth Press, 1998, pp. 85-124.

23. Dickstein, Ruth, et al. From Zero to Four: A Review of Four New Women's Studies CD-ROM Products, In: Kristin H. Gerhard, ed. *Women's Studies Serials: A Quarter-Century of Development.* New York: The Haworth Press, Inc., 1998, pp. 59-84.

24. Dobson, Cynthia, Kushkowski, Jeffrey D., and Gerhard, Kristin H. A Collection Evaluation for Interdisciplinary Fields: A Comprehensive Approach. *Journal of Academic Librarianship* v. 22 (July 1996), pp. 279-84.

25. Coutts, p. 287.

26. Johnson, Peggy. Collection Development Policies and Electronic Information Resources. In: G.E. Gorman and Ruth H. Miller, eds. *Collection Management for the 21st Century.* Westport, CT: Greenwood Press, 1997, p. 87.

27. Coutts, p. 285.
28. Lee, p. 178.
29. Ackerson, Linda G. Visualizing the Configuration of Scientific Literature: A Study of Disciplinary Relationships. *Reference & User Services Quarterly,* v. 39, no. 1 (Fall 1999), p. 43.
30. Ackerson, p. 49.
31. Gorman, Michael. Ownership and Access: A New Idea of Collections *College and Research Libraries News,* v. 58, no. 7 (July/August 1997), p. 499.
32. Coutts, p. 288.
33. Buckland, Michael. What Will Collection Developers Do? *Information Technology & Libraries,* v. 14 (September 1995), p. 158.
34. Buckland, p. 158-9.

Collection Development in the New Millennium– Evaluating, Selecting, Annotating, Organizing for Ease of Access, Reevaluating, and Updating Electronic Resources

Virginia Baldwin

INTRODUCTION

The literature of the early 1990s suggested changes in the structure of collection management itself in order to accommodate the changes both now occurring and those foreseen. Sheila Creth wrote in 1991 "Until recently, the primary focus of collection development has been on building collections."[1] She outlined the functions of collection management in academic libraries to include: selection of materials, weeding, preservation, liaison with faculty and academic departments, reference and user education, fiscal responsibility, and policy development. Creth saw the necessity for a basic change in the library's organization structure. "According to the principles of organizational design, the traditional structure of the university library is functional in nature . . . Change has become the common denominator for the university library."[2] Therefore, Creth called for a collection management team structure of subject librarians with subject expertise to provide the basis for accommodating these changes. In 1989 Atkin-

[Haworth co-indexing entry note]: "Collection Development in the New Millennium–Evaluating, Selecting, Annotating, Organizing for Ease of Access, Reevaluating, and Updating Electronic Resources." Baldwin, Virginia. Co-published simultaneously in *Collection Management* (The Haworth Information Press, an imprint of The Haworth Press, Inc.) Vol. 25, No. 1/2, 2000, pp. 67-96; and: *Electronic Collection Management* (ed: Suzan D. McGinnis) The Haworth Information Press, an imprint of The Haworth Press, Inc., 2000, pp. 67-96. Single or multiple copies of this article are available for a fee from The Haworth Document Delivery Service [1-800-342-9678, 9:00 a.m. - 5:00 p.m. (EST). E-mail address: getinfo@haworthpressinc.com].

son[3] foresaw the need to soften the emphasis on division of responsibilities by subject in favor of subdividing subjects according to functions. The functions suggested by Atkinson were notification, documentation, instructional, historical, and bibliographical. These correspond to five information sources:

1. Notification sources–journal articles and monographs written by scholars for other scholars.
2. Documentation sources–all primary materials. These will differ by discipline.
3. Instructional sources–summaries of knowledge such as textbooks or manuals.
4. Historical sources–sources that may be needed one day for historical research.
5. Bibliographical sources–those that organize and provide access to the other sources.

In the year 2000 and beyond, we can most certainly see an impact from electronic resources on all five functional areas on Atkinson's list, with historical sources being an especially elusive one considering the ever-increasing quantity of non-archived electronic information. Creth's team approach is one frequently used as we see more and more libraries tackle the function of providing organized access to web resources using teams consisting of subject librarians, computer specialists, educational technologists, and graduate students.

In early 1995 a group of librarians from the University of Michigan School of Information developed a virtual-library, called the Internet Public library in response to the proliferation of unorganized resources on the World Wide Web. This event marked a breakthrough team response to rapidly developing changes in the information world. During this time period OCLC created the "NetFirst" database as a way to provide bibliographic records for Web sites.

Responses to the Internet began long before these dramatic developments. Back in the days before gophers were available we telnetted to information sources and used ftp to download. When gophers were developed, we began to organize gopher sites for our patron's use. It soon became clear, as Susan K. Martin noted in her 1996 article on organizing Internet collections, that to ignore the world of electronic materials in collection development would be to "ignore an increasingly large proportion of the knowledge of any discipline. . . . Users

Virginia Baldwin 69

should know that a particular electronic resource has been examined and identified as appropriate for their library 'collection' by the same person who selects their books and journals . . ."[4] And, by the way, as Martin proposes, we need to keep the same statistics for these resources that we keep for traditional resources.

This chapter tracks the methods that members of the library profession have devised to deal with new electronic resources and with the continuous change in software developments to manage them. While not every individual library or librarian has managed immediate assimilation of these changes as they have occurred, as a profession we have dealt with them admirably. The question is whether or not a time will come when a sort of equilibrium is reached–a time when our libraries are organized enough in the electronic realm so that new developments will require only a modicum of accommodation.

SHALL WE GO FOR THE GOPHER?

The University of Minnesota developed the Gopher computer software in 1992. Soon, like their biological counterpart, Gophers began springing up in libraries everywhere. A useful tool for organizing Internet access points in a hierarchical structure, Gophers were soon used to link library patrons with external information sources such as catalogs from other libraries, as well as internal directories and databases, such as, in the case of Eastern Illinois University, to the school newspaper, the *Daily Eastern News* in electronic format. The Gopher allows the user to seamlessly telnet, download, and break connection, thereby enabling movement from one source to another with just the pressing of an arrow key or the appropriate letter key and the enter button. A "/" at the end of a line indicates that the line is a category that will lead to another hierarchical tree of sites.

The hierarchical structure of Gopher enabled Librarians to begin to organize sites by categories, and collection development librarians soon found themselves wanting to use the software to provide organized subject access to article databases, electronic journals and other electronic resources, library catalogs and local resources. In 1993 Lieberman and Rich noted, "New and innovative approaches are already redefining the way information specialists retrieve, organize and disseminate information."[5]

Early on, the issue of access versus ownership became a trouble spot. It was difficult, given the traditional librarian mindset, to provide pointers to information sources over which there was no control. Providing "access to electronic journals without downloading files and maintaining local archives . . . represents a major philosophical shift for libraries that borders on an abdication of their primary mission."[6] With the decision not to archive, however, came the obligation to regularly verify that the remote archive is being maintained and kept active. Additional problems associated with pointing rather than downloading and archiving include down servers at the site pointed to and pointers eliminated from a remote Gopher.

Draper Laboratory Library implemented a Gopher in January of 1994 through a team effort between Library and Computer Services personnel. Because of the inherent disorganization of the Internet's resources, Draper Library customers looked to the library to provide a simple organized method of access to this Internet information. The librarians involved were reticent about launching the Gopher until the menu structure was perfected and included the most appropriate set of resources. In an article about the Draper Gopher, Rotman, Spinner, and Williams of Draper Laboratory described how the team reconciled a problem continually experienced in the realm of Internet Resource Collection Development. "By its very nature, however, gopher is always evolving. We could have kept adding new resources and adjusting the menu structure indefinitely and it still would not be perfect. We eventually realized that it was better to launch the gopher, receive feedback from end-users and make adjustments as we continued the process."[7]

Another important issue that is well remembered by those of us who sought to organize resources using Gopher is that of where specifically in a remote Gopher site we should establish a pointer. Should we merely point to a remote site and then let the user find the gems that are accessible from that site, or rather, point to the individual title level, be it a document, file, newsletter, etc.? Probably we are derelict in our duties as collection development librarians if we do the former. This is expressed admirably in "The Internet and Collection Development: Mainstreaming Selection of Internet Resources" regarding Gopher development at Cornell University's Mann Library "We believe that title by title selection of high quality resources is one of the most important values librarians can add in providing access to information resources including those accessible via the Internet. A careful selection of resources is the touchstone of the electronic library."[8]

Two subject specific Gophers were produced at the National Library of Medicine (NLM) to provide organized access for both internal and external resources.[9] The TEHIP (Toxicology and Environmental Health Information Program) Gopher was implemented as a result of a long range planning panel issued in September of 1993 and the AIDS Gopher was initiated in response to discussions that occurred at a conference in June of 1993. After addressing issues of stability, reliability, and currency of information, developers considered numerous organizational issues. Structures given consideration included the separation of NLM resources from non-NLM resources, separation of resources by producer, separation of resources by subject terms, such as Medical Subject Headings, and separation of resources by format (files, Gophers, listservs, etc.). Each Gopher entry is limited to 70 or less characters of text. Therefore, an explanation of the organizational philosophy of the Gopher occurred in a text file accessed from the first item on the main menu of the Gopher.

Another issue to be addressed by the NLM Gopher was the number of levels of menus that could be presented without causing the user to get lost in the Gopher. Is it better to list a large number of items on a single menu or to have short menus with many levels to get to an information source? Two things were clear, that it was best to (1) create menus that can be viewed on a single screen and (2) have multiple pathways to the same source levels. Other organizational considerations were given by Grajek and Marone. "Standardize menu features in fixed positions because consistency is important. For example, information about the gopher could be in the first position, searching in the second, etc. The most important and frequently used items should be higher up in the menu. Include a top-level menu of shortcuts to the most popular services, such as telephone directories, schedules of events and the library catalog and databases, since this facilitates access to them."[10]

These are the kinds of organizational concerns, which were addressed, in the early 1990s by librarians everywhere who were dedicated to providing their patrons with extensive access to this new world of electronic resources. In 1994 the University of California, Irvine "Virtual Reference Collection" of Internet resources included one of the most frequently consulted gopher resources, called the

"Virtual Reference Desk" which was designed and maintained by a librarian. This site and its organizational structure became the basis for a Web-based Virtual Reference Collection.[11]

Still true today, even back in the gopher age the question was being raised as to why "so many libraries and schools (were) creating gophers that all link to the same Internet information."[12] "The need is not just for access to information, but for access to organized and well-maintained information"[13], so why not pool resources so that each piece of information is organized and maintained by only one librarian? A case in point is the Oregon Online Project for the State of Oregon.[14] The Gopher for this system is browsable at *gopher://gopher.state.or.us.* Designed around an automated document management concept, the project volunteers were from 25 different state agencies. The difficulty here was obtaining agreement from the contributors as to the topical hierarchy and on a standardized document format. The outcome was an automated cooperative development of information sources on a Gopher.

Internet usage increased dramatically at Yale in October 1993 when their gopher was formally announced. The "greatest draw for external users seems to be not local information but our organization and maintenance of links to external information."[15] As their portion of the contribution of several universities who are "voluntarily apportioning maintenance of global gopher resources, . . . Rice University and Michigan State University maintain a list of subject trees gleaned from searches of discipline-specific gophers at more than a dozen institutions."[16]

On the other hand, from a librarian's perspective, the value of a locally established library gopher may lie more in its uniqueness rather than the collaborative efforts that may have produced it. Quite possibly, the dramatic changes that ensued may have occurred before any kind of a compromise was reached, but a locally modified gopher that had been collaboratively established may have been a workable solution and the best of both worlds.

One of the downsides of the Gopher hierarchy is that movement through the trees to the eventual location of a site of interest required either a remarkable memory for subsequent return to the site, or lengthy recording of linking information. This was soon resolved with a bookmarking capability that was available to each individual user. For the user with his or her own computer, now a personal, individualized organization structure was available for more convenient access to frequently used sites.

Two other network access tools of note that were developed in the early 1990s are LIBS from Mark Resmer at Sonoma State University and HYTELENT from Peter Scott at the University of Saskatchewan, Canada.[17] Both provide seamless telnet access to numerous OPAC's, databases, information services, and campus-wide information systems. HYTELNET does not have the subject-based approach to accessing information resources that LIBS had. The LIBS software could be downloaded by anonymous FTP and customized for local usage. The main menu of on-line services available through the Internet had six entries. The first two entries were for library catalogs in the United States and other countries. The next three were for information systems, services, and access tools. The last was information for first time users of the program.

Most of the information in the next menu level was in alphabetical order. As an example, the second menu level under Databases and Information Services was topical in organization and included six broad areas such as Business, Education, Science and Weather, and a 7th area, Other.

HYTELNET[18] is still available as an http protocol site. In 1997, Peter Scott announced the discontinuation of its maintenance. Figure 1 depicts the main screen of the Hytelnet Web site "HYTELNET on the WorldWideWeb" (*http://www.lights.com/hytelnet/*).

FIGURE 1. Portion of the HYTELNET Web Interface Main Screen as of December 1999

Search | Suggest | What's New?

* Library Catalogues, arranged geographically
* Library Catalogues, arranged by vendor
* Help files for Library Catalogues
* Other Resources

* Sites using the Java(tm) Telnet Applet
* Internet Glossary
* Telnet tips
* Telnet/TN3270 escape keys
* Link to webCATS: web-based online catalogues
* Link to Publishers' Catalogues Home Page
* Librarians Resource Centre
* HYTELNET is closing down!

Librarians everywhere were realizing the value of providing access to these gophers along with access to their OPACs and electronic databases. One way to provide access was to set the client's default "home" gopher to a designated gopher site. Another was to establish a gopher bookmark. With the advent of browsers and the proliferation of electronic indexes, abstracts, and full text databases, librarians have devised ways to direct the patron to resources appropriate to his or her needs. Methods of organizing electronic resources have become increasingly sophisticated as librarians have merged networked CD-ROM databases with telnet resources and added full text databases, electronic journals, and basic Internet resources as each of the these formats has become available. Ways of presentation of these resources vary with libraries. Libraries have attempted to organize these resources by subject areas, by full text versus citation and abstract only, by monographic versus serial titles and other methods.

BOOKMARKING

The introduction of Mosaic, developed in 1993 at the National Center for Supercomputer Applications (NCSA), a research institute at the University of Illinois, brought about the obsolescence of gophers. At first we traced through web links with consternation and near disbelief. What were we to do now? While hyperlinking made accessing a site remarkably easy after the experience of telnetting and following gopher links, how were we to have any organized structure for accessing sites that were useful in our subject areas and for Reference work? Soon bookmarking of web browser URL's appeared and there was optimism again, until we had an unmanageable string of bookmarks. Then, along came bookmark folders (for Netscape Navigator and Favorites for Internet Explorer). We were not certain if we should be thankful or worried that someone might be taking over our jobs.

Problems and resolutions continued to abound. In 1996 when access to electronic journals as part of digital library projects was being structured, Barber acknowledged a difficulty with using bookmarking to facilitate the monitoring of the "arrival" of new journal issues.[19] Ideally, bookmarking could be used to bring up the site page that lists journal issues available. This would make it relatively easy to check to see if a new issue had been released. However, many publishers did not maintain this information on static web pages, and in some cases, access to these sites were as part of a searching session, causing access by bookmark link to bring up a session expired notification.

In "Never Lose Sight of Your Site," Terrence Young suggested using folder names that parallel the subject headings in the library catalog. Young furthers the analogy by saying that Bookmarks and Favorites are similar to the catalog records. Among the software described in this article is Smart Bookmarks which "automatically checks Web sites and proactively notifies you not only when something has changed, but also tells you what has changed. . . . Using Smart Bookmarks you can import existing bookmarks, add custom descriptions and comments to bookmarks, define categories and folders, and move bookmarks from one folder to another."[20]

For Mac users, there is Macuser's Site Seer that keeps track of every site visited and creates drag-and-drop-aware windows for bookmarks. WordPerfect has a filing system named Cardfile that can be used to create discipline specific files for organizing URL's. The files can be "filled" by copying and pasting.[21]

Another major milestone, reached in mid-1993, grew out of a file of some 750 bookmarks that was started in 1990 as a gopher bookmark file by Carole Leita at the Berkeley Public Library (BPL). BPL mounted a web site on the City of Berkeley's new web server as the "Berkeley Public Library Index to the Internet." In March of 1997 the BPL index moved to the UC-Berkeley Digital Library SunSITE and the Librarians' Index to the Internet (LII) was born. The LII is both searchable and browsable, with over 40 major categories that are modified Library of Congress (LC) subject classification categories and cross-references.[22] Organizing the Internet began to take on a new meaning. Figure 2 shows the categories on the home page of the site (*http://sunsite.berkeley.edu/InternetIndex/*).

TAXONOMIES OF INTERNET RESOURCES

Because of the great variety of types and formats of Internet resources, many librarians have developed schemes especially designed for organizing these resources. In early 1993, four librarians at Cornell University's Mann Library began a project of selecting Internet resources of potential interest to library clientele.[23] Librarians at Cornell found that "the development of classification schemes (is) a powerful

FIGURE 2. Categories of Links on the Librarians' Index to the Internet Main Screen as of December 1999

Subscribe: - New This Week -
More new... - New Last Week

Arts - Architecture | Museums | Performing | more...
Automobiles - Motorcycles
Business - Investing | Taxes | more...
California - Politics | Bay Area : Berkeley | Oakland |
San Francisco | Southern California : Los Angeles
Computers - Software | Viruses | more...
Cultures (World) - Anthropology | Africa | Asia | Europe | Lat A | MidE | NorA
Current Events
Disabilities
Education - Distance | K-12 | Colleges | Aid | more...
Families - Homes | Moving
Food - Recipes | Restaurants | more...
Gay, Lesbian, Bisexual
Geography - Maps | more...

Government - Federal | International | more...
Health - Diseases | Nutrition | more...
History - Genealogy |
Ancient | Medieval | Military | U.S.
Images, Graphics, Clip Art
Internet Information - Filtering | Evaluation | Training |
WWW | more...
Jobs - Listings | Resumes | more...
Kids - Fun | Health | Homework | Internet Safety | Parents
| Teachers
Language - English | Spanish | more...
Law - Censorship | Copyright | Crime | more...
Libraries - Public | for Librarians
Literature - Authors | Genres | Prizes | Publishers |
more...
Media - News | Magazines | Newspapers | Radio | TV
Men
Music - Jazz | Lyrics | Opera | more...
Organizations

People - Collected Biographies
Philosophy
Politics - Elections
Recreation - Games | Gardening | Movies | Guide
| more...
Reference Desk - Calendars | Census | Dictionaries |
Holidays | Homes | Phone Books | Statistics | Tim
Religion - Christianity | Islam | Judaism | Mytholo
more...
Science - Animals | Astronomy | Environment | M
Technology | more...
Searching the Internet - more...
Seniors
Sports - Baseball | Olympics | Tennis | more...
Surfing the Internet
Travel - Accommodations | Places | Transportatio

Weather - Tides | more...
Women - History | Politics | Studies

tool in adapting the principles of collection development to new forms of publication" (p. 281). Mann Library employed a "genre" model for selecting electronic publications to allow the grouping of resources into logical units of analysis in order to focus staff expertise on certain information types. In doing this, a taxonomy was devised to categorize Internet resources into 15 categories and 21 subcategories. Categories included reference, monographs, serials, gophers, gateways, literature and book reviews, graphic images, sound, videoconferences, and selection tools. The resulting taxonomy was strongly reflective of Mann Library's particular subject interests. However, developers "found that overall the process of devising and working with such a classification scheme was an invaluable exercise in thinking through (their) . . . approach to Internet selection.

"Grouping titles into taxonomic categories enabled us to evaluate and compare, from a collection development perspective, a set of resources with similar characteristics."[24] Furthermore, this intellectual process served to clarify the selection criteria for collection development of Internet resources.

OCLC took the approach of cataloging Internet resources in ways similar to its traditional cataloging system. In 1996, with its First-Search system of databases of article indexes now enjoying widespread acceptance, OCLC added a new database, NetFirst, composed strictly of records of web resources. Each record was in traditional FirstSearch format, was retrievable through a standard search, and consisted of author, title, subject, abstract, and other fields. A second OCLC project, the Internet Cataloging project (*http://www.oclc.org/oclc/man/catproj/catcall.htm*) was funded by the U.S. Department of Education and it began in 1994. Librarians from 231 libraries created its MARC format records.[25]

Anne Callery, cataloger at Yahoo! Inc., described the Yahoo! Approach to Web site organization at the "Untangling the Web" conference in Santa Barbara, California.[26] When Yahoo! created its subject directory its founders realized that as a stand-alone resource of strictly Internet sites, there was no need to integrate its sites with other long-standing resources. Therefore, Yahoo! founders devised its own classification system. Furthermore, because of the changeable nature of the Internet object being cataloged, it made no sense to create anything as structured and complex as a MARC record. Furthermore, they reasoned, access to a site was so easy compared to a trip to the stacks that the user could just as easily jump in and make a decision about the usefulness of the contents of a given Web site. Basically, the person who submits a site to Yahoo! suggests a category. The subject hierarchy for Yahoo! is a "bottom up" approach, since it is dictated by whatever is submitted, with new subcategories often being created as a result of a submission. Yahoo! does have a structure for regional divisions, and all commercial sites are added under Business and Economy, in either Companies or Products & Services. Yahoo! accesses sites only at the top level of a document, or its significant sections. A Web search engine, on the other hand, may pull up dozens of resources within one given site. Figure 3 depicts The Yahoo! Subject Directory hierarchy.

Perhaps the obvious alternative to the MARC record of traditional library resources and the "bottom up" approach of Yahoo! is the creation of a core of metadata elements specifically created for tagging Internet and other electronic resources. Just such an effort began in March of 1995 at a Metadata Workshop sponsored by OCLC and the National Center for Supercomputing Applications, and attended by librarians and other relevant professionals from a dozen countries. The result was the Dublin Core element set of initially 13, since expanded

FIGURE 3. The Yahoo! Subject Directory Hierarchy as of December 1999

Arts & Humanities
Literature, Photography...

Business & Economy
Companies, Finance, Jobs...

Computers & Internet
Internet, WWW, Software, Games...

Education
College and University, K-12...

Entertainment
Cool Links, Movies, Humor, Music...

Government
Elections, Military, Law, Taxes...

Health
Medicine, Diseases, Drugs, Fitness...

News & Media
Full Coverage, Newspapers, TV...

Recreation & Sports
Sports, Travel, Autos, Outdoors...

Reference
Libraries, Dictionaries, Quotations...

Regional
Countries, Regions, US States...

Science
Animals, Astronomy, Engineering...

Social Science
Archaeology, Economics, Languages...

Society & Culture
People, Environment, Religion...

to 15 core elements: title, creator, subject, description, publisher, contributor, date, type, format, identifier, source, language, relation, coverage, and rights (management).[27]

The 15 elements or metatags, "when implemented, form the Internet's equivalent of a bibliographic record for electronic documents. . . . The idea is that the author or creator tags electronic documents according to a set of standards. . . . The search engines then need to be able to retrieve documents according to these metatags."[28] Younger called for libraries to "identify incentives to encourage information creators and producers to incorporate standard metadata in their publications . . . (such as) copyright or patent registration (incentives and) revenue derived from increased access."[29]

The search engine INFOMINE began as a list of Web sites at the University of California, Riverside. Its entries are organized with modified LC subject headings and University of California librarians select the web sites (*http://infomine.ucr.edu*). There are nine basic subject areas and each subject area has five browse features, "What's New," "Table of Contents" (browse by subject and title), "Subject," "Keyword," and "Title." The heavily funded Scout Report (*http://scout.cs.wisc.edu*) is housed in the Computer Science Department of the University of Wisconsin. Those reports that are cataloged are done so with LC. Since library classification doesn't necessarily translate to the Internet, a new classification system is under investigation. Michigan Electronic Library's[30] Sue Davidsen is wary of traditional Dewey and LC classification since they were created for a physical object shelved in a physical location. Some of the many predictions and proposals for an individual library's approach to organizing information sources include multi-tiered approaches, replacement of URL lists with distinct records with annotations, creation of an Internet subject thesaurus and subject gateways. One of many Multi-tiered schemes was suggested by cataloging expert Michael Gorman:

1. Full cataloging
2. Enriched Dublin core records
3. Minimal Dublin Core records, and
4. Reliance on unstructured full-text keyword searching.

For the information community as a whole, foreseen are automating functions and some melding of various methods of cataloging and access.[31]

In 1991, the Committee on Institutional Cooperation (CIC, a consortium of the members of the Big Ten athletic conference plus the University of Chicago) created a protocol for mining the Internet for electronic journals and organizing them onto a gopher site for easy access. Journals were organized alphabetically by title and also by subject. Initially, only freely distributed electronic journals were included in the collection (now a web site at *http://ejournals.cic.net/*). This was a boon to librarians for it allowed them to include the CIC URL and a brief description of what was contained therein to give immediate and organized access to a wealth of free scholarly journal articles in a variety of subject areas.

In 1993, University of Michigan librarians created dozens of pathfinders on a gopher site, then organized them by subject areas on the University of Michigan server at *http://www.lib.umich.edu/chhome. html*.[32] This site became the Argus Clearinghouse, a widely used subject directory and search engine for the Internet.

In November of 1995, Cyberstacks(sm), an organization of significant science and technology resources on the Internet using first level LC Classification, was formally established on the home page server at Iowa State University (*http://www.public.iastate.edu/~CYBERSTACKS/ homepage.html*). Cyberstacks(sm) offers the following "main menu":

G Geography, Anthropology and Recreation
H Social Sciences
J Political Science
K Law
Q Science
R Medicine
S Agriculture
T Technology
U Military Science
V Naval Science

Currently, J, K, U, and V are not linked to Web resources. A second tier of organization is available for the remaining LC Classification schedules, for example, for Q, which is the only class that at the time of this writing has links to all second tier classes (twelve classes, QA through QR). At the next tier under these secondary headings LC Classification subjects and number range are given for each of the twelve levels, but contain links to Web resources for only selected ranges.

Cyberstacks(sm) also has a cross-classification index which is a subject listing in alphabetical order, and, in response to preliminary user feedback, each resource was incorporated into a newly created Title Index in 1996. The Title Index contains all resources that have been assessed including those which have not yet been described, categorized or classified, or otherwise fully integrated within the collection.[33] An icon distinguishes between the two levels. The record for each categorized website in Cyberstacks(sm) is formatted according to the Web site information depicted in Figure 4.[34]

Out of Great Britain came an organization of resources by Dewey Classification *http://bubl.ac.uk/link/*. Known as BUBL LINK, or LINK, all resources are catalogued using the Dewey Decimal Classification (DDC). On the main screen many organizational approaches are available for the catalogued sites. In addition to a link to "Dewey," there are links to a search engine, to a hierarchical alphabetical list by

FIGURE 4. Record Format for Cyberstacks(sm) Categorized Web Site

---

Record Format

We have attempted to provide the following categories of information about each selected resource, in the order indicated:

1) Specific Library of Congress Classification
2) Resource Title/Name
3) Full and Correct URL
4) Record Summary

   a) Subject Coverage
   b) Resource Size/Number of Entries
   c) Record Structure
   d) Special Features
   e) Miscellaneous Notes
   f) Source Acknowledgement

5) Search Instructions
6) Preferred Form of Contributor's Name and Affiliation

For each record summary, when and where possible, we have excerpted the summary data from the original resource to provide sufficient information about its subject coverage, and other features, to enable users to judge a resource's potential usefulness.

subject ("subject menus") which leads through the Dewey classification scheme to cataloging records of sites, and "countries" which does the same for sites relative to a given country. There is also an alphabetical link to subjects through links to letters in the alphabet. Each resulting record contains the following basic elements: Title, Description, Author, Subjects, DeweyClass, ResourceType, Location, and, occasionally, Date last checked.

Also on the initial screen is the Internet-subject-directory-appearing list of topics and subtopics that do not correspond to the structure of the DDC. However, each topic or subtopic leads hierarchically to cataloging records of sites (and these *are* classified according to the DDC).

CyberDewey   (*http://ivory.lm.com/~mundie/CyberDewey/CyberDewey. html* is another site that lists Internet sites that are organized using the Dewey Decimal Classification scheme. It consists of a listing of the 10 classes and one hundred divisions of the DDC with the number of links under each division given in parentheses after the division.

In addition to Cyberstacks(sm), Iowa State University is home to another site, "Beyond Bookmarks: Schemes for Organizing the Web," that is compiled and organized by Gerry McKiernan (*http://www.iastate. edu/~CYBERSTACKS/CTW.htm*). This site lists classification systems and controlled vocabularies that are used on the Web, and provides links to sites that employ them. Among the classification systems listed are Alphabetic, Numeric, Engineering Information Classification Codes, Mathematics Subject Classification, Universal Decimal Classification (UDC), Alphanumeric, Library of Congress Classification, and National Library of Medicine. Among the controlled vocabularies listed are Library of Congress Subject Headings, Medical Subject Headings, and National Library of Medicine.

More recently, in 1997, the Northern Light[35] search engine took a completely new tact by creating a scheme to allow users to "narrow" their initial search by choosing from among a set of folders created at the time of the search to represent concepts that reoccur within the documents retrieved. Librarians developed the keywords or categories depicted by the folders. The term "custom search folder" is trademarked and NorthernLight patented the process. Figure 5 depicts the 1st and 2nd tiers of folders that result from the search "Kolb learning cycle" and the selection of "Teachers and Teaching" from the 1st tier.

The Internet Quick Reference (IQR), called "A Seamless Web-based Library" by its developer, Steve Weiss,[36] a Document and

FIGURE 5. NorthernLight 1st and 2nd Tier of Folders for the Search Kolb Learning Cycle as of December, 1999

Your search returned 451 items which we have organized into the following Custom Search Folders:
  Search Current News
  Teachers & Teaching
  Higher education
  Educational sites
  Careers & occupations
  Education theory & research
  Parent involvement in education
  Psychology
  Teaching methods
  Psychology of learning
  Multiple intelligences
  Class notes & Assignments
  all others . . .
US Patent 5,924,090
	Your search returned 94 items which we have organized into the following Custom Search Folders:
	  Teachers & Teaching
	  Special Collection documents
	  Teaching methods
	  Class notes & Assignments
	  Educational sites
	  Personal pages
	  univnorthco.edu
	  asee.org
	  purdue.edu
	  2learn.ca
	  ntlf.com
	  northern.edu
	  umuc.edu
	  all others . . .

Reference Librarian at Utah State University, contains Internet links that are organized in a table of contents. The site is browsable in the sense that the table of contents and the annotated links to which its elements point are all downloaded upon entry into the site. Included are links to sites of particular value to Utah State University library patrons, and to some that are only available to those patrons. Figure 6 shows the Table of Contents on the main screen (*http://cc.usu.edu/~ stewei/hot.htm*).

In late 1998, OCLC began a third Internet project when it announced plans to begin the Cooperative Online Resource Catalog (CORC) project (*http://www.oclc.org/oclc/research/projects/corc*).

As a response to the thousands of individual library attempts to provide lists of web links deemed useful to their patrons, OCLC's CORC is designed to facilitate cooperative development of these individual efforts. "CORC's objective is to provide the infrastructure support so that libraries can build the gateways automatically."[37] But, we are jumping ahead. Let us now look at some of these gateway-building and other individual organizing activities.

LIBRARIANS ORGANIZING WEB LINKS FOR PATRON ACCESS

"The Internet has changed the concept of 'place' in relation to both collections and collectors. In the electronic world, it has become less

FIGURE 6. Table of Contents on the Main Screen of the Internet Quick Reference as of December 1999

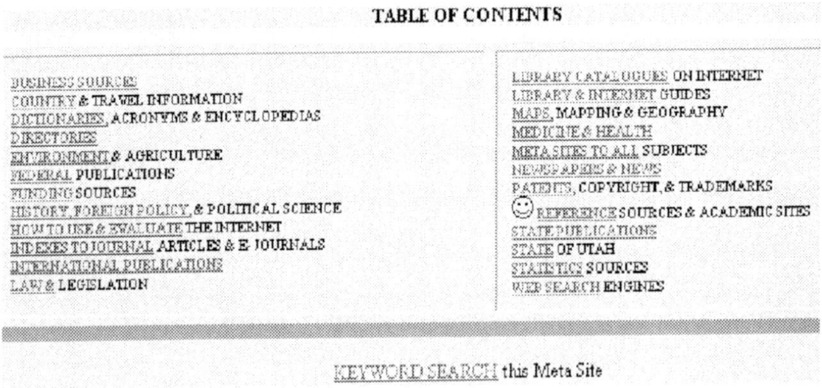

TABLE OF CONTENTS

BUSINESS SOURCES	LIBRARY CATALOGUES ON INTERNET
COUNTRY & TRAVEL INFORMATION	LIBRARY & INTERNET GUIDES
DICTIONARIES, ACRONYMS & ENCYCLOPEDIAS	MAPS, MAPPING & GEOGRAPHY
DIRECTORIES	MEDICINE & HEALTH
ENVIRONMENT & AGRICULTURE	META SITES TO ALL SUBJECTS
FEDERAL PUBLICATIONS	NEWSPAPERS & NEWS
FUNDING SOURCES	PATENTS, COPYRIGHT, & TRADEMARKS
HISTORY, FOREIGN POLICY, & POLITICAL SCIENCE	☺ REFERENCE SOURCES & ACADEMIC SITES
HOW TO USE & EVALUATE THE INTERNET	STATE PUBLICATIONS
INDEXES TO JOURNAL ARTICLES & E JOURNALS	STATE OF UTAH
INTERNATIONAL PUBLICATIONS	STATISTICS SOURCES
LAW & LEGISLATION	WEB SEARCH ENGINES

KEYWORD SEARCH this Meta Site

important WHERE a document resides and more important to have reliable, well-organized (and presented) access to it. We want to know who produced it, who identified it as valuable, and who selected it for our use, but that person does not have to sit at the desk next to us. We no longer need to 'own' a physical manifestation of the information in our private institutional domain, but we must provide the appropriate technological and organizational infrastructure to access it reliably."[38]

Several approaches have been taken to dispense information about useful web sites to library patrons. Reference librarians together with subject specialists and often computer technology personnel have organized front-end menus that provide access to the library's OPAC and article databases, their internal resources and CD-ROM's, as well as Internet links and links to electronic journals available either through subscription or those with free access. Hypertext subject guides are proliferating in a variety of forms, breadth, and depth of inclusion. Most include Internet links considered valuable for the subject area. More and more of these links include annotations of contents, response time, disclaimers given, and other information about the site as well.

As lists of links grew larger, they began to require lengthy scrolling through screen after screen to view the entire list. So, librarians began to organize the links in various ways, resulting in a variety of diverse schemes almost as large in number as the number of libraries employing them. As we browsed through other web sites we found ever better ways to organize these links, and contemplated or produced these sometimes massive changes.

In "Finding Our Way," Kathleen Kluegel describes the all-too-frequently occurring experience of navigating through layer-upon-layer of menus, only to find we've gone down the wrong path and must backtrack and try another path. She suggests the tourist guide analogy, with "multiple modes of access: a spot for direct entry of a title if it is known; a list of resources for those who would recognize the name of the needed resource; a functional choice for those seeking resources of a particular type; as well as a more guided selection process."[39]

Very often a frequently linked site will have a very useful internal link. Annotating and providing a separate link for this internal element can make all the difference to the harried patron.

In "Netting Political Science–Finding Resources on the Web," Lucia Snowhill gave numerous examples of Internet link organization. For sites listed in the international relations subject area, some link arrangements were by source, type of information, topics such as area studies, economic development human rights, documentary sources, major theorists vs. political theory, etc. and annotations included information about these types of arrangements.[40]

The categories of links appear to be endless. Department links, links to links and/or gateways from other libraries, preprint sites, associations, listservs, "other" formats, newsletters, e-journals appropriate to the subject areas, links to lists of print resources for various types of reference sources, and links to databases appropriate to the subject area are some of the more common categories of links. All of the categories in the Mann Library taxonomy, mentioned earlier have undoubtedly been used at various sites.

Going back to our initial look at library organization, many issues become relevant. Should there be a standard template for organization of subject specific sites?

Gateways

The web-based OPAC is a candidate for the library's gateway to Internet resources. Libraries everywhere have begun using the Electronic Location and Access (856) field of the USMARC record to provide links to electronic resources that have been purchased through standard and cooperative acquisition processes. Some libraries have begun to include free resources that have been selected by collection development specialists. Many questions surround these practices. Links can be provided to the electronic (Internet) versions of books, and this can be done regardless of whether the book is available in print in the library. Refer to Chapter 10 in this book for Tom Peters' discussion of the rapid development of computer networks and digital scholarly and academic information resources. In regard to electronic journals, the issue is whether the OPAC link would be to the Internet address of the journal publisher, to a separate file of online journals, or whether the record will be hotlinked to the full text.[41] In fact, a fourth possibility is to provide a link to the publisher's journal search screen for those publishers who provide that capability.

Furthermore, serials cataloger Amanda Xu may have the ultimate solution in the eventuality of a successful Dublin Core type tagging of Internet resources.[42] She considers the possibility of a library OPAC serving both as a gateway to Internet metadata repositories and to its existing databases. Then she goes on to say that library systems can harvest this metadata and she discusses the potential for developing a library metadata conversion system. In fact, the Internet is approaching the size that will make it necessary to have indexing done only on document metadata rather than the document contents because of the enormous number of documents on the Web, with no end of the proliferation in sight. Xu "analyzes a library metadata conversion system that will be able to extract selected incoming external metadata from Internet resources, convert it into USMARC format, and integrate it with existing library databases *automatically*" (p. 195).

Regina Reynolds in "Inventory List or Information Gateway? The Role of the Catalog in the Digital Age,"[43] concluded that the shift that is occurring from the catalog as inventory list to information gateway was both inevitable and desirable and that the cataloging record must make it clear to the patron whether or not the title is actually owned by the library. Reynolds also discussed a Library of Congress initiative to develop a cooperative archiving of electronic journals to which individual libraries could point in their OPAC's, as opposed to pointing to the publisher's web site.

But apart from the predictable and possibly justified aversion of librarians to catalog and place on their OPAC an Internet resource that may be here today and gone tomorrow, or changed so substantially as to require recataloging, there are other reasons to provide separate, organized, lists of links to Internet resources, in addition to those that are provided on subject-specific Web sites. Many of these reasons can be classified under the heading of Potential Ways A Patron Might Seek Access To A Library Recognized Web Site.

Library gateways abound. Often they are embedded in a set of headline links. A whole chapter could be written on a taxonomy of library gateways. One thing a library gateway can do that an OPAC search may not (at least not yet) be able to give us is a link by subject to a list of records of electronic-only resources. This is the converse of Reynolds' suggestion "searching strategies should allow patrons to limit searches to a base catalog of items actually owned by the library."[44] Both approaches are valuable organizational access methods and do not supplant each other.

The aforementioned Committee on Institutional Cooperation (CIC) site was one of the first comprehensive, organized listings of electronic journals. From its beginnings as a gopher site in 1991, it gave both subject and title browse lists. Figure 7 depicts the Electronic Journal Collection menu that has not changed since its inception. The "Topic Browse" listing was by broad subject categories that arose from the subject areas represented by the journals available. Their web page states, "Ultimately, this collection aims to be an authoritative source of electronic research and academic serial publications–incorporating all freely distributed scholarly electronic journals available online. The CIC-EJC serves as the electronic journal collection for the CIC member university libraries. The collection is fully cataloged by the CIC member libraries, and records are contributed to the international bibliographic database OCLC. Ultimately, the collection will include

FIGURE 7. Committee on Institutional Cooperation Electronic Journal Collection Menu as of December 1999

electronic serials licensed only to the CIC member universities, and access to licensed publications may be restricted under the terms of the applicable license agreements. . . The CIC-EJC is a collaborative initiative between the librarians of the CIC member universities, CIC-Net, and the CIC Center for Library Initiatives."[45]

A very useful and much referenced gateway to electronic journals comes from the Colorado Alliance of Research Libraries. Figure 8 shows the search entry and the various links on the main screen. These links include alphabetical indexes by title and LC Subject Heading, two very useful organizational schemes. The link to "Other Directories of Electronic Journals" provides an annotated list of more than twenty sites that contain listings of electronic journals, including those from CIC and BUBL. Also useful are the "Directory of major publishers of electronic journals" and "Use this form to recommend new titles for inclusion" both of which are useful for locating new titles to be added to the electronic journal list.[46]

The most thoughtfully designed gateways and the most highly linked OPAC cannot, however, overcome the many problems that the user will find upon arriving at a site. Barber identifies several. Once the patron clicks on a link the result may be one or more of the following:

1. Service at the site is temporarily unavailable.
2. Technical capabilities at the site may be inadequate.
3. The interface at the new site most likely will be unlike any ever before encountered.
4. Full-text searching or browsing will apply only to a limited set of articles.[47]

The aggregation of Internet resources and journals from multiple publishers at one site will alleviate some of these problems. Is this strictly a publisher function? What kind of a role can the librarian have in making this a reality? Recently, three publishers announced the establishing of an agreement to provide hot links to each other's cited articles. These hot links would only be activated to full text at a site where the patron has established access. This is progress.

FIGURE 8. Colorado Alliance of Research Libraries Gateway to Electronic Journals as of December 1999

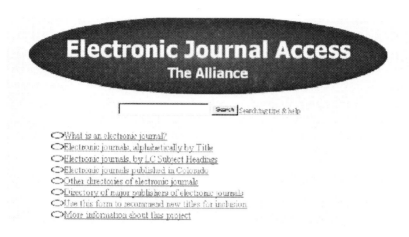

THE EMERGING ROLE
OF COLLECTION DEVELOPMENT LIBRARIANS

The "here today, gone tomorrow" phenomenon of Internet sites is somewhat mollified by software available to check links. An example is the free link checker, NetMechanic.com, which may be used at some regular frequency to ensure all hotlinks are active. This, however, does not relieve the webliographer of the necessity to periodically look at each site linked to make certain the contents continue to be appropriate for the use to which they have been put. For a site to be adequately maintained, new links can be added when discovered, usually through sources such as listservs, library publications, books, etc. That is, until "the evolving information technology makes it obsolete–replaces it with something better–perhaps a hand-held, artificial intelligence voice recognition system which accesses a world of information from a universal database of knowledge" (U.S. Dept of Commerce, 1999).[48] In his article, "The Seamless, Web-Based Library: A Meta Site for the 21st Century," Weiss describes Web design considerations, many of which take on the magnitude of new and distinct roles for the librarian. In addition to all the organizational considerations, the librarian can take on a marketing role. The Web site can be registered with a search engine like Yahoo!. Other such sites can be found through what else, but an Internet search. Other advertising methods mentioned by Weiss are a referral service like *http://Recom-mend-It.com*, contact with other Webmasters for mutual linking, and announcing on appropriate listserves.[49]

All of the preceding sections of this article make it clear that collection development librarians must not only keep abreast of new technologies, they must also learn about emerging technologies and predictions of them. Although we have coped admirably with changes as a profession, individually we have been inconsistent at best in using the various organizing tools that have come along for electronic resources.

Some thoughts for the evolving future of librarians' relationship with electronic resources:

- Eventually, we may find that all computers will act as host computers in the future evolution of resource organization. All formats and types of information will be divided among the community of users and librarians for evolving and continual addition of resources to that collective universal database of knowledge using an all-encompassing classification scheme. OCLC's CORC effort is analogous to this. Never fully realized with gopher, now we have the possibility of global and cooperative evaluation, annotation, and classification of resources accompanied by local selection and modification to accommodate local patron needs.
- While librarians and others have been developing a multitude of classification schemes, others are working on natural language processing and voice recognition systems. If Microsoft's Natural Language Processing (NLP) engine were "used as a Web-search engine, a user could enter a query and have a reduced number of responses, unlike current search engines."[50]
- We have been amply forewarned, even back in 1996. "By the end of the decade" (the arrival of perhaps 500,000 electronic serials will raise the question of) . . . "How will this new and potentially enormous and pervasive medium be integrated into existing structures of information organization and brokering? Libraries will be the key to the success or failure of electronic scholarly publishing. With proper proactive management, the success of this new medium will benefit both libraries and the academic community. However, if the academic community and libraries

fail to take the initiative in the development of this new medium, then we will be faced with a budgetary and organizational nightmare that may lead to an increased drain on declining acquisition budgets."[51]

• "For the first time in over 200 years, the paper scholarly journal can be supplanted, or at least, supplemented in a significant way by the rise of network-based electronic journals and that this may lead to a new type of scholarly discourse. . . . I think that a paradigm shift in the process of scholarly discourse is on the horizon and that this will be accompanied by a fundamental shift in the technological basis of academic communication and publishing."[52]

• "Librarians are certainly destined to play a key role in disseminating the publicly funded and freely accessible electronic scholarly information when, for the first time in history, we will have a seamless interface between the university and the community. This university-community interface will take the form of a supernetwork of community Freenets that are linked to the larger academic Net and thereby have direct access to the growing wealth of electronic information resources created by and for all peoples. Hopefully the current trends in network-based electronic publishing will continue in such a way that will foster the speedy arrival of such an information system."[53]

• The issue of database design and user interfaces becomes more critical as our library becomes more virtual. "Our users will demand an interface that is intuitive, easy to navigate, and dynamic; one that provides a uniform gateway for the services offered by the virtual library.

"Will our current library instruction screens and tutorials evolve into a more complex system of instructional design? Will we become instructional designers as well, or at least become part of an instructional design team, perhaps composed of both librarians and (instructional design professionals)."[54]

Link Personalization

Our personal computers come with their own Internet organization system in the form of browser bookmarks. If we download Netscape, we receive an initial set of bookmark folders with it. In version 4.7, those folders are "Search, Directories, Banking and Finance, Business Resources, Computers and Technology, Education, Entertainment,

General News, Hobbies and Lifestyles, Local Information, Shopping, Sports, Travel and Leisure and My Stuff." Is this a clue to the ultimate in resource organization and access? To quote Ken Winter in "My Library Can Help Your Library," "The promise of personalization in library settings is two-fold: First, it can help save librarians the hassle of creating countless and redundant Web pages, which are much harder to maintain than they are to create. And who can honestly say the pages they've created make sense to most end users? After all, a Web page designed for everyone must necessarily incorporate a least-common-denominator approach, making it simplistic for experts yet still confusing to novices. Second, personalization allows for incredibly detailed target marketing of your library's staff, services, and resources based on such factors as patrons' unique interests, the types of sources they use most, their academic major, or any other factor that seems relevant."[55] Yes, personalization to be most effective can and will be done at the individual level, to include even the faculty and every undergraduate in a large university. In his article Winter describes many such efforts being undertaken at various universities, including North Carolina State, Calpoly San Luis Obispo, Cornell, and UCLA. At UCLA, close to 100% of a student body of over 35,000 students have created a My.UCLA (*http://my.ucla.edu*) Web page and the pages are heavily and regularly used. With these site personalization resources, patrons can visit their site from their dorm or any other location. Their favorite sources will be arranged in a way that is most useful to them. Alerts can be provided not only of new journal issues, but also of new books in their field.[56]

Can we, as librarians, ultimately expand this personalization scheme to include the electronic journals and academic sites that will be needed for the research interests of every library patron whether they be students, faculty, staff, or administration? We have seen so much arrive and be supplanted in the decade of the 1990s. We have created and embraced new approaches to information organization to the benefit of our patrons. Perhaps all that we have done will become obsolete. Perhaps it *will* lead us to a kind of equilibrium, one that will enable us to concentrate our efforts more on changes in the flow of scholarly information and new challenges in instructional design. In so doing, we will be more able to constantly keep the most useful information sources readily available to our patrons and teach them how best to access and use them.

NOTES

1. Sheila Creth, "The Organization of Collection Development: A Shift in the Organization Paradigm," *Journal of Library Administration* 14, no. 1 (1991): 73.
2. *Ibid.* p. 70-71.
3. Ross Atkinson, "Old Forms, New Forms: The Challenge of Collection Development," *College and Research Libraries* 50, no. 5 (1989): 507-20.
4. Susan K. Martin, "Organizing Collections Within the Internet," *The Journal of Academic Librarianship* 22 (1996): 291.
5. Kristen Liberman and Jane Rich, "Lotus Notes Databases: The Foundation of a Virtual Library," *Database* 16, no. 3 (1993): 33.
6. Donnice Cochenour and Thomas Moothart, "Relying on the Kindness of Strangers: Archiving Electronic Journals on Gopher," *Serials Review* 21, no. 1 (1995): 69.
7. Laurie Rotman, Margaret Spinner, and Julie Williams, "The Draper Gopher: A Team Approach to Building a Virtual Library," *Online* 19, no. 2 (1995): 21-28.
8. Samuel Demas, Peter McDonald, and Lawrence Gregory, "The Internet and Collection Development: Mainstreaming Selection of Internet Resources," *Library Resources and Technical Services* 39, no. 3 (1995): 280.
9. Gale A. Dutcher and Stacey J. Arnesen, "Developing a Subject-Specific Gopher at the National Library of Medicine," *Bulletin of the Medical Library Association* 83, no. 2 (1995): 228-33.
10. Susan Grajek and R. Kenny Marone, "How to Develop and Maintain a Gopher," *Online* 19, no. 3 (1995): 37.
11. Ellen Broidy, Kathryn Kjaer, and Christina Woo, "Untangling the Tangled Webs We Weave: A Team Approach to Cyberspace," in online conference proceedings *Untangling the Web*, Santa Barbara: University of California, Santa Barbara, available at *http://www.library.ucsb.edu/untangle/broidy.html*. The "Virtual Reference Collection" at *http://www.lib.uci.edu/home/virtual/virtual.html* refers to the "UCI Research Resources A-Z" and gives the link *http://www.lib.uci.edu/rraz/genref.html*.
12. Susan Grajek and R. Kenny Marone, "How to Develop and Maintain a Gopher," *Online* 19 no. 3 (1995): 41.
13. *Ibid.* 41.
14. Ernest Perez, "Oregon Online," *Database* 18, no. 6 (1995): 32-40.
15. Susan Grajek and R. Kenny Marone, "How to Develop and Maintain a Gopher," 41.
16. *Ibid.* 42.
17. Deidre E. Santon and Todd Hooper, "The LIBS Internet Access Software: An Overview and Evaluation," *The Public-Access Computer Systems Review* 3, no. 4 (1992): 4-14.
18. Peter Scott, "HYTELNET As Software for Accessing the Internet: A Personal Perspective on the Development of HYTELNET," *Electronic Networking* 2, no. 1 (1992): 38-44.
Figures in Scott's article show snapshots of files in the early HYTELNET software. The first version was released in early 1991. Screens from Version 6.2 are captured in Scott's article "Using HYTELNET to Access Internet Resources" in *The*

Public-Access Computer Systems Review 3, no. 4 (1992): 15-21 at *http://info.lib.uh.edu/pr/v3/n4/scott.3n4*.

19. David Barber, "Building a Digital Library: Concepts and Issues," *Library Technology Reports* 32, no. 5 (1996): 573-701.

20. Terrence E. Young, "Never Lose Sight of Your Site," *Book Report* 17, no. 1 (1998): 34.

21. Mary N. Hernandez and Karen Daziel Tallman, "Untangling the Web: Using the World Wide Web for Art and Humanities Reference Services," in online conference proceedings *Untangling the Web*, Santa Barbara: University of California, Santa Barbara, available at *http://www.library.ucsb.edu/untangle/hernandez-abs.html*.

22. Norman Oder, Holly Hinman, and Carole Leita, "Cataloging the Net: Can We Do It?," *Library Journal* 123, no. 16 (1998): 47-51. The origin and operation of the Librarians' Index to the Internet LII is described by founder Carole Leita with Holly Hinman in a sidebar to this article. The sidebar is entitled "A Public Librarian Helps Launch an Index."

23. Samuel Demas, Peter McDonald, and Lawrence Gregory. "The Internet and Collection Development: Mainstreaming Selection of Internet Resources" 275-290.

24. *Ibid.* 281.

25. Norman Oder, Holly Hinman, and Carole Leita, "Cataloging the Net: Can We Do It?" 49.

26. Anne Callery, "Yahoo! Cataloging *the Web*," in online conference proceedings *Untangling the Web*, Santa Barbara: University of California, Santa Barbara, available at *http://www.library.ucsb.edu/untangle/callery.html*. The URL for Yahoo! is *http://yahoo.com*.

27. The Dublin Core element set, version 1.1, is defined and described at *http://purl.oclc.org/dc/documents/rec-dces-19990702.htm*. A formal standard for the description of metadata elements is used.

28. Cherrie Noble, "Reflecting on Our Future: What Will the Role of the Virtual Librarian Be?" *Computers in Libraries* 18, no. 2 (1998): 50-54.

29. Jennifer Younger, "Resources Description in the Digital Age," *Library Trends* 45, no. 3 (1997): 468.

30. The Michigan Electronic Library (MEL) home page is available at *http://mel.lib.mi.us/*.

31. Norman Oder, Holly Hinman, and Carole Leita, "Cataloging the Net: Can We Do It?"

32. The URL *http://www.lib.umich.edu/chhome.html* currently links over to the Argus Clearinghouse site at *http://www.clearinghouse.net/index.html*.

33. Gerry McKiernan, "Casting the Net: The Development of a Resource Collection for an Internet Database," in online conference proceedings *Untangling the Web*, Santa Barbara: University of California, Santa Barbara, available at *http://www.library.ucsb.edu/untangle/mckiernan.html*.

34. Cyberstacks(sm). The title list within Cyberstacks(sm) is available at *http://www.public.iastate.edu/~CYBERSTACKS/title_lst.htm*. The record format description is available at *http://www.iastate.edu/~CYBERSTACKS/record.htm*.

35. NorthernLight.com. Available at *http://www.northernlight.com*.

36. Steve Weiss, "The Seamless, Web-Based Library: A Meta Site for the 21st Century," in American Society for Information Science conference proceedings *Knowledge Creation, Organization and Use* (Medford, NJ: Information Today, Inc., 1999) 47-55.

37. Ron Chepesiuk, "Organizing the Internet: The 'Core' of the Challenge. (Dublin Core Metadata Element Set)," *American Libraries* 30, no. 1 (1999): 62. This quote is a portion of a quote by Chepesiuk of OCLC Senior Research Scientist Stuart Weibel.

38. Charlene M. Baldwin and Steve Mitchell, "Collection Issues and Overview," in online conference proceedings *Untangling the Web*, Santa Barbara: University of California, Santa Barbara, available at *http://www.library.ucsb.edu/untangle/baldwin1.html*.

39. Kathleen Kluegel, "Finding Our Way," *RG* 36, no. 2 (1996): 172.

40. Lucia Snowhill, "Netting Political Science–Finding Resources on the Web," in online conference proceedings *Untangling the Web*, Santa Barbara: University of California, Santa Barbara, available at *http://www.library.ucsb.edu/untangle/baldwin1.html*.

41. Cindy Stewart Kaag, "Collection Development for Online Serials: Who Needs to Do What, and Why, and When," *The Serials Librarian* 33, no. 1/2 (1998): 107-22.

42. Amanda Xu, "Metadata Conversion and the Library OPAC," *The Serials Librarian* 33, no. 1-2 (1998): 179-98.

43. Regina Reynolds, "Inventory List or Information Gateway? The Role of the Catalog in the Digital Age," *Serials Review* 21 (Winter, 1995): 75-77.

44. *Ibid.* 77.

45. Barbara McFadden Allen, "The CIC-EJC as a Model for Management of Internet-Accessible E-Journals," *Library Hi Tech* 15 no. 3-4 (1997): 45-49. Quote is from the Committee on Institutional Cooperation "CIC Electronic Journals Collection" Web page [accessed December 1999]. Available at *http://www.cic.net/cic/*.

46. Colorado Alliance of Research Libraries, *Electronic Journal Access The Alliance*. Available at *http://www.coalliance.org/*.

47. David Barber, "Building a Digital Library: Concepts and Issues," 630.

48. Stephen C. Weiss, "The Seamless, Web-Based Library: A Meta Site for the 21st Century," 49. Weiss quotes the U.S. Department of Commerce National Telecommunications and Information Administration (NTIA) (1999) conference report "Technology Trends: Options for the Future" in U.S. Dept. of Commerce. NTIA. *Society & Information Infrastructure: The Next Generation. 1998 Networks for People.*

49. *Ibid.* 51-52.

50. Jeff Walsh, "User Interfaces Crumble on Net," *InfoWorld* 19, no. 45 (1997): 131.

51. Michael Strangelove, "Current and Future Trends in Network-Based Electronic Journals and Publishing," in *The Evolving Virtual Library: Visions and Case Studies*, ed. Laverna M. Saunders (Medford, NJ: Information Today, Inc., 1996), 143.

52. *Ibid.* 143.

53. *Ibid.* 144.

54. Cherrie Noble, "Reflecting on Our Future: What Will the Role of the Virtual Librarian Be?" 51.

55. Ken Winter, "MyLibrary Can Help Your Library," *American Libraries* 30, no. 7 (1999): 65.

Ibid. 65-67. For more information on this type of resource, visit the University of Washington University Libraries' MyLibrary Project, "My Gateway" at *http://www.lib.washington.edu/resource/help/MyGateway.html.*

Collection Development and Organization of Electronic Resources

Gerald L. Newman

INTRODUCTION

Historically, collection development librarians concerned themselves with selecting resources to be added to the collections. After its acquisition, catalogers controlled the material through the catalog. The nature of electronic resources has caused collection developers to be more involved in the issues of organization of resources for best presentation to, and access by, users. While organization and access were, of course, functions of the catalog, different expectations come into play in the world of point-and-click. Not only has delivery of information to the libraries changed, so too has the ability of users to get to resources through other ways than the traditional catalog, even its current electronic database incarnation.

This paper investigates the importance of the organization of electronic resources, especially as it requires input, subject expertise and time of selectors or bibliographers. Among other issues, it investigates different publication types and resource packagings. It discusses traditional access through the catalog, as well as access to electronic resources through the web. It discusses different web pages, including system-wide, library, discipline or subject specific. It touches upon purchased resources, as well as resources available freely, and deals

[Haworth co-indexing entry note]: "Collection Development and Organization of Electronic Resources." Newman, Gerald L. Co-published simultaneously in *Collection Management* (The Haworth Information Press, an imprint of The Haworth Press, Inc.) Vol. 25, No. 1/2, 2000, pp. 97-113; and: *Electronic Collection Management* (ed: Suzan D. McGinnis) The Haworth Information Press, an imprint of The Haworth Press, Inc., 2000, pp. 97-113. Single or multiple copies of this article are available for a fee from The Haworth Document Delivery Service [1-800-342-9678, 9:00 a.m. - 5:00 p.m. (EST). E-mail address: getinfo@haworthpressinc.com].

97

with who sets policy on how resources are organized, as well as who does the actual work. The academic library is considered to be the focus of the discussion. Within that focus are multi-library, multi-campus environments, as well as issues for members of consortia.

NOT JUST SELECTION

The advent of electronic resources has brought about many changes within libraries. Resources, services and job assignments have all changed in many ways. Within the realm of collection development, organizing resources has taken on an enhanced level of importance. Before electronic resources, a selector was concerned with expending a budget and did so by choosing appropriate titles for purchase. Often this might entail research and active choice. At other times, selection might be more passive or automatic. In either case, however, after selection, control of the title moved to other personnel in the library. Typically, acquisitions purchased the title and catalogers put the title through appropriate bibliographic controls and entered it into the library's database of titles.

Electronic resources, especially those delivered via the web, have complicated that simpler routine. Now the question of post-selection control is of greater importance. For selectors, this is not simply a matter of shifting time from selecting resources to organizing them. Selection still goes on. Budgets still need to be spent. Librarians charged with collection budgets still have the responsibility of choosing resources appropriate to their situation. In some cases, however, the purchase decisions now involve a large gathering of resources, frequently with much higher costs than in the past. Along the way subject selectors have added various responsibilities in the newer arena of organizing these resources both in relatively traditional ways as well as in entirely new ways. And while bibliographers or selectors may have assisted in control questions before, their role in this area has expanded dramatically. This expansion, of course, adds to the pressures of varying tasks competing for time. Time spent to improve access to resources is time that needs to be shifted from other tasks. There are several factors that contribute to putting organization of resources high on a list of priorities.

INCREASED IMPORTANCE IN THE ORGANIZATION OF RESOURCES

Several major reasons come to mind when one examines the need for increased focus on organizing library resources:

1. There is the need to provide better access through the information overload with which users are faced. This is especially true in the world of electronic resources where issues of quality and quantity raise different hurdles. The Internet provides access to huge numbers of pages of information. Consistent quality, however, is not what one finds.
2. There is the technical possibility of bringing together a fuller, richer mix of available resource types to bear on a user's query. Different types of resources can easily be brought to bear on the same question and come seamlessly to the user's workstation.
3. Importantly, there is the responsibility to provide direct and efficient access to large, extensive and increasingly expensive resources.

IMPORTANT ISSUES IN THE ORGANIZATION OF RESOURCES

While the numbers of resources have expanded dramatically, so have their formats and methods of access. This variety further complicates the task of providing best access. Several of the factors include:

1. Types of resources
2. Organizational methods available
3. Logic and attractiveness of presentation
4. Ease of access
5. Policy makers
6. Implementers
7. Environment

The interplay of these factors calls more and more for the skills and experience of the subject selector whose knowledge of the subject field, the intended users and the relationship of the pieces can inform the organization.

TYPES OF RESOURCES

The Monograph

As one contemplates the move of resources to electronic format, the first thought is not of the monograph. It comes to the table somewhat later than other resources. Nonetheless, electronic books, that is, single subject full-length monographs are available in their entirety electronically. They are available fully, complete with flexibility unachievable in paper monographs. There are, of course, electronic means to do simple computer tasks like word searches through an entire text or portions of the text. There is the ability to cut and paste portions of the text into other documents. Tables of contents and indexes can be used to move efficiently through a monograph. For example, an index can have hot links to occurrences in the text to which it refers. This type of flexibility can be particularly useful for resources to which users would want to refer rather than those from which they might read long text passages.

Traditionally, of course, monographs have been controlled in the libraries' databases. In the current electronic environment, that is, of course, still an option and a desirable event. The existence of web catalogs, however, allows for much more. A link can now be made directly from the catalog entry to the resource, allowing users smooth, direct access.

Full Text of Serial Titles

Serial titles have become available electronically. In many cases, users have access to the title cover-to-cover. Individual serial titles have traditionally been controlled in the libraries' cataloging database, and their availability electronically has done nothing to change the fact that they can be cataloged in much the same manner as before. However, with the addition of a web catalog, these titles too can be accessed directly with a link from the catalog. Frequently a link can take a user directly into the title where he or she can navigate through issues and articles, as appropriate.

Aggregates of Full Text Serial Titles

Another of the more recent electronic arrivals has been the packaging of groups of journals which are available virtually cover-to-cover.

In some of these services, fairly recent information is available. *Project MUSE*[1] comes to mind. In others, the purpose of the aggregation is to provide retrospective coverage of the titles included. Here *JSTOR*[2] is an example. Both are services wherein serial titles are available cover-to-cover electronically for some portion of their publication history. Once again, traditional treatment in the library database is a beginning step in control and access to these services. On the surface of the issue, cataloging the aggregate title would not appear to be very useful. Who, in fact, would be seeking the information contained in either *Project MUSE* or *JSTOR* with the aggregate title? Yet cataloging the aggregate title should direct users to at least a description of the service and its content. Cataloging all the titles within the service would seem to be a more worthwhile task, as it would give more direct access to the individual parts of the aggregate. And in the web catalog, all the individual parts of the service could be accessed by direct link. This appears to be a good step, with each periodical title getting specific bibliographic control. On the other hand, cataloging the title of the aggregate too can in fact be quiet useful, as these aggregates can be databases in their own right, with their own search engines and search capabilities which allow cross-title searching within their own universe. As one might suspect, a simple description of the service would fall short of fullest and best access to these resources. The web catalog, of course, allows for a link to the service, including its database and its search engine. Therefore, patrons wanting to search this specific service are led to the appropriate point where they may be allowed to enter a search and get a result. Then, in fact, instead of entry into a chronological run of issues of titles available in full text, patrons can be pointed to specific articles within those titles that have a relation to their specific query. This more pointed access to specific article level information nearly makes the journal title and its run irrelevant, the retrieved article being the desired object.

Indexing and Abstracting Databases

At the beginning of the electronic era, among the most important first services were major indexing and abstracting services. In fact, they continue to be major players in the electronic equation. They provide their own interesting challenges and opportunities in the endeavor to get best control of, and access to, resources. Cataloging the database itself allows a user access to the fact that the resource is

available. Typically, however, the subject control over the database title is necessarily broad, too broad in many cases to be useful. However, a link from a web catalog can bring the database to the user's fingertips. From there, the user can do searches typical of that particular database, including those employing very specific subject, author, title or keyword strategies. The capabilities of the particular database will determine how accessible its internal information will be. The end result is that the user will retrieve a list of references to articles. But possibilities go beyond what the database itself provides. Many providers of these services now provide links to the holdings of the user's library. In the world of paper titles, links to holdings, of course, show the user which titles are in the library's holdings, most likely with the holdings specified from the library's database. In the more electronic mode, the link might also point directly to the electronic journal, or perhaps the specific article from the journal, which the user has found in the index and to which the library has a subscription.

Databases with Full Text

Perhaps the most complicated among electronic resources are those databases that not only index or abstract but also contain full text either for all or some of the material indexed by the database. At minimum, as with the sources mentioned above, the title of the database can be entered into the library's database with appropriate cataloging. Very often, of course, the name of the database might be irrelevant or unknown to a potential user. So this approach has limitations. The database, which might be very broad indeed, also has but one set of subject headings to describe its nature. Once again this is often a very broad approach and is of limited help to a user. Of course, if the user finds or knows the title through the catalog or in another way, a link from the catalog may be made to provide direct access to the database. Once again, the database's own internal capabilities become operative at this point. The user retrieves relevant material, some of which might be full text and provided directly by the database provider to the users. The rest of the retrieved material might be in the form of citations to sources not available in full text by that provider. Should this database provide links to holdings, a user would be able to find in a fairly simple manner whether or not the library subscribes to the title in question. Of course, if the title is an electronic one with an electronic link, access might be directly to the title or to the specific article. Except for initial discovery of the database and it relevance, a user might have success getting satisfaction from this method. The library's problem, however, especially in the case of full-text avail-ability to texts within the database to which the library has no sub-scription, is how to indicate to users at large that there is access to these titles through this particular database. Instead of pointing from a vendor product, say an abstracting source, to journals held by the library, the library is trying to point its users to access it has in a vendor product. The vendor, of course, is in control of the database. Potential problems here are numerous. For example:

1. The titles may be covered full text but not for a significant period of time
2. The full text may be to articles only with other portions of the journal material excluded
3. Parts of the same journal issue may not all be added at the same time, and
4. Inclusion in the database may be fluid. The provider may have a limit on how long material stays within the database or may have a weighted scale to be variously applied to different types of re-sources within its database.

Appropriate control and access require investigation and decisions concerning, at minimum, questions of importance, reliability, stability and maintenance. Without some indication of access to these titles, the library is not using its resources as fully as possible.

TYPES OF RESOURCE ORGANIZING

In the above discussion of resources types, reference was made to some of the possibilities for dealing with bibliographic control and access issues. For many years, the library has had the card catalog and its successor, the library electronic database, at the center of its attempt to control material. With good cataloging of resources, and, as neces-sary, assistance from public service staff, patrons had a fair chance of getting to appropriate resources. The bulk of effort was directed to-ward cataloging books and serials. To be sure, there were also micro-form and audiovisual resources controlled in a similar fashion. There were other aids to the library's endeavor. There were, and still are, periodical indexes and abstracts. There was cataloging for large microform sets.

In the current electronic environment, librarians still hold the library's central electronic catalog to be central to the organization of materials. They still expect that, whenever possible, resources will be available through it. They also endeavor to make as many connections as they can through current web catalogs. They lobby providers to include a mechanism to link to holdings. Nonetheless, there are now other means available to their use. Ironically, these means allow users to completely circumvent the one resource into which librarians have invested so much energy and focus, the library's own database.

WEB PAGES

The Internet and the development of web pages have become a recent focus for organization and presentation of resources. With accelerating speed, the Internet has become not only a fascinating communication tool, but also a major information directory and repository. Web pages proliferate with amazing speed and with many purposes. Among these are academic sites, along with many of their services, including the library. Library databases have been available for years, at first as specific dialup sites allowing access to the catalog alone. With more sophistication, web pages began to describe services and then resources, often linking to that prime resource, the library database. Then with increasing sophistication, libraries soon began to put up other important resources allowing ease of access while removing the walls of the library as boundaries. This immediately brought organization decisions and principles to the attention of those hoping to provide best organization and access to resources.

Because the web is a place of freedom and ingenuity, individuals and institutions approached web pages in a variety of ways, often reflecting the skill development of particular individuals. The very individual approach of a selector creating a specific page related to a specific subject without a major framework within which it fit was often the beginning. At the other end of the spectrum was the library beginning with a general page, including many general, and perhaps specific, resources on it. And while the individual mentioned might not have fit within a framework of a library-wide page, many would say that the ability of this page to come forth on its own is a specific glory of the Internet. It is not necessary to fit into specific historic moulds to succeed. Logical hierarchies and relationships may be completely ignored to present a specific focus on a web site. As time progressed, more and more institutions moved to have both the general sites, with ever-increasing complexity along with the many individual subject specific pages, pointing to narrower focuses.

While freedom and flexibility is still a trademark of the web, many library sites have become increasingly complicated. The individual page of the individual selector can still be found with specific information relative to a limited portion of the world of knowledge. Often, but not necessarily, it is now part of a larger collection of sites related to resources in the library. These sites may or may not have the appearance of belonging to a hierarchy. In some ways this flies in the face of library organization heretofore. The question of recreating a different way to access the resources of the library implies a great amount of overlapping work. While it is true to suggest that the catalog is limited in its ability to describe adequately, for example, major, mixed databases, the development of many disparate web sites creates new work of different sorts. Ironically, this development may also detract many users from the full array of resources available through the catalog, in effect, by bypassing it entirely.

WHICH WEB SITES–FROM THE NARROW TO THE BROAD

Many library organizations have seen the benefits of creating fine web sites and providing access from them to many of their resources. I have suggested only two pages thus far. They are the individual selector's single subject page and the library-wide resource page. In fact, there are many combinations and permutations in the web page scenario. The single selector and his or her page may focus on only one narrowly focused subject. On the other hand, the page may bring together disparate subjects that would not otherwise be seen as belonging together simply because of a selector's library responsibilities or subject expertise. Of course, the rationale for some of these clusters would be less than obvious to users.

The creation of a subject page has as one of its major purposes the gathering and highlighting of specific focused resources at the library's disposal which might serve a user doing research in that area. In its creation, decisions need to be made. Are only narrow, very subject-specific resources to be included? The negative here is that the approach leaves out the less focused but broader or related resources. The user then has to go elsewhere to find those resources. Does the page go for the broader approach, including many related resources, and thereby risk loss of focus and lean toward overkill? Where is the happy medium and who decides it? Because the page is often the child of the selector, direction is a personal and professional decision. But, as its purpose is likely to be the organization of resources for a specific narrower field, the inclination might be to use the narrower approach. Clearly, organization commissioned or determined by the library professional responsible for the area makes great sense. As this person is also the selector of resources, the liaison with the faculty in that area, and perhaps instructor and facilitator for that portion of the collection, there is the potential for this page to do great service for the library users of this subject collection. In addition to link selection, the organizer can establish a layout that directs patrons. Added annotations or descriptions can be as lengthy as necessary to describe the resources. The creator is not limited by Library of Congress subject descriptors. The selector needs to decide whether or not to include information from other library web pages, including the highest level general, or all-inclusive, pages. All of the decisions are in the page creator's hands.

Library-wide pages also have been developed and here the emphasis tends to be on broad coverage of library resources. It is here where emphasis may be broad and inclusive. Library-wide web pages would be likely to attempt to gather together all the electronic resources of the varying fields. The possibilities include gathering all resources by type. For example, a link to a listing of all the indexing and abstracting databases or to all the electronic journals available to patrons might be typical. The web site format once again allows more flexibility than the library's database, but it makes necessary a whole array of questions. And of course, in the process, adds an entire layer of relatively new work to the library organization. Arrangement of the above-mentioned examples of collecting resources can take several forms. The databases could be arranged alphabetically by title. That is a clear and simple way to organize resources. Of course, it assumes users will know the names of databases that are appropriate for their information needs. A different option is to arrange the database titles by subject. This necessitates the creation of a subject list appropriate to the library's collection, user base, or university campus structure. Then comes the assignment of each database title to the appropriate subject or subjects. There will be some of very broad interest that will need to be put in many categories. In actuality, many libraries will decide to do both an alphabetical list and a subject list. The same decisions would need to be made for resources such as electronic journals, that is, alphabet and subject arrangements, again, all requiring new decision structures. Selectors will be among those contributing to these efforts.

We have discussed the individual selector pages by subject, as well as library-wide pages. These are but two ends of a possible spectrum that might also include broad subject discipline pages or pages anchored in a library branch other than the general library on campus. These pages might encompass several specific subjects and partake in some of the characteristics of narrower, subject-focused pages as well as providing broader cross-disciplinary information. There might be pages organized around broad disciplines such as the humanities or the social sciences. There could be pages focused on a cluster of related fields or subject libraries on campus, as in science pages that might have as their center one or more of the programs available within the university.

WHO DECIDES

As suggested above, people with the interest, time and technical capabilities developed the earliest web pages. Beginning with gopher pages and evolving to web pages took special interest, time and skill. Many of those who had these skills envisioned a new way of presentation and had independent views of how scenarios might play out. Of course, as the interest and the necessity of more advanced web pages became evident, so too did the need to coordinate what was happening among many individuals. While it was often still possible for many individuals with subject pages to have autonomy over those pages, it became evident to many that the broader pages had information that could be used effectively on subject-focused pages. Broad links to all the library's available databases or all its electronic journals might be seen to be valuable on any page. In fact, their absence would be a disservice to the user.

Coordination among web pages of varying levels then became more important and continues to operate in university libraries in varying degrees. Selectors and public service staff, often the same people, needed to give input on questions of relationships among resources and on questions of hierarchies and best access. In this newer world, libraries have not abandoned the library's cataloging database. The catalog is still at this point the sine qua non of organization, though its attendant routines needed to be adapted somewhat to electronic resources. Instead of being part of the physical delivery process that brought materials into the building, processing units now need to be advised of titles coming in electronically. It now is incumbent upon the organization to have clear routines established so this information finds its way to the appropriate personnel.

As electronic resources proliferated, committees or task forces were required to make various policy decisions concerning treatment. How would new resources be treated? Cataloging of a database, though woefully inadequate from some perspectives, was a start. How far did one go to catalog titles within a database? In some cases, as in the *Project MUSE* and *JSTOR* examples above, rationale for cataloging titles within them was fairly clear, as the title was complete, cover-to-cover, and from an apparently stable source. On the other hand, how far should cataloging proceed on vendor products which provide information that is far less stable? Here links to holdings within the library's database were a different solution, in effect, providing more direct information about how the database's universe was covered in the library holdings. This at least gave improved access to resources, as well as to information resources not owned by the library.

With the web catalog, there came questions of linking resources to the database. Linking, of course, requires yet more time and skill, a new workflow in the processing units, to make it possible for users to have direct access. What things should get linked? Should everything that can be linked actually be so treated? Are there certain categories where this should be done and others where it should not, or perhaps be done selectively? Again, task forces or groups of interested personnel needed to be formed to make rules. Typically, this involved individuals from the processing units, public service and collection development.

As various groups meet to discuss policies for getting control of the new processes, there are concerns that the good parts of the new model of organizing resources not be too tightly constrained by new boundaries. On the other hand, there are valid concerns about making sites fit academic models. Sites should surely highlight important resources available to users. They should surely allow, as possible, a simple click to access the resource. They might involve an academic or teaching tone, not only pointing to resources, but also offering instruction on access or use at the same time. They might also provide a clear path from the general to the specific in research, not unlike a pathfinder.

Ease of access should be a raison d'être of the pages, of course. As coordination takes place, the look of an individual page is seen to be part of the larger site. Attempts might be made to make pages look and function in a similar fashion, to give them the same "feel." While an individual may balk at encroachments on his or her manner of expression and organization expressed in a page, it is true that a page creator needs to be aware that users moving throughout a site should be able to find their way as easily as possible. Pages with an entirely unique approach can provide a jarring disorientation to the user. Similar organization shared across pages minimizes disorientation and speeds recognition. This after-the-fact coordination among pages can also be a top-down approach not only to make pages look and work the same way but may also be an attempt to get reluctant participants to join the fold. For example, collection development librarians may be influenced by their supervisor to join the other internal library pages that successfully organize and lead users to important and expensive resources. Questions of functionality and appearance are of importance here so the library may appear to be a center of coordinated effort in regard to resources, their organization and their use.

WHO DOES THE WORK?

New decisions concerning electronic resources need input from a variety of people, including the collection development librarians. Selectors finding a way to organize the resources of their specific fields may in fact have begun individual pages. They were most likely involved in decisions about links from the web catalog. And their input was essential for discussion about library-wide sites, and their relation to individual subject sites and perhaps interim levels. So too was their input necessary for discussions about coordinating internal library web sites, especially those facilitating resources available to users. Who does the work from this point on? Do professionals do the actual work on their own pages? At a very functional level, this is already possible with user-friendly software. On the other hand, is it the most appropriate use of their time? How do we create and maintain sites for selectors who may be less technologically adept? Do we give them help? Is this yet another balancing act of skills and needs within the library organization? And once created, who monitors the pages and all their links to keep the pages current. Technology can help here, but only partially. It will still be necessary to view the pages with a selector's eye to see that they are accomplishing what they were intended to do, and in fact, what they are capable of doing in the new environment.

ENVIRONMENTS

There has been discussion above about single subject web pages. In some ways they might be seen as single strands in the new web of pages. There has also been discussion of the library-wide web pages and the complexity introduced when the attempt is made to gather together all of one type of resource for ease of access. There was also the suggestion of interim levels of pages, each showing its own kind of complexity: the broad subject page and the separate page for a separate library entity, most often focusing on a specific subject. Cases can be much more complicated in reality. The simplest scenario in university libraries would be to have the above mix within one large central library that comprises its own entire system. The larger the university, the more likely it is that this simple reality does not exist. Subject focused libraries may exist on campus and complicate the equation. It has already been suggested that libraries of this type require different answers to web resource organization questions. In fact, even though these libraries may belong to the same administrative structure of the rest of the libraries, they may be strongly related to the department or school or college they serve. The relationship may be strong enough that the library is pulled to emulate the web pages of that entity rather than the central library page. An answer may be to take the look of the related entity to show affinity, but as a service unit with its own imperatives, to take the form of the library's pages, as possible. In other words, look like the related academic unit pages, but function in presentation and logic, as related library pages.

Still further apart are the more independent types of branches, that is, those that report to different chief librarians. The typical examples here would be law libraries and medical libraries, though others exist. These units are more autonomous and have more specialized functions. This makes the need and the desire to cooperate less evident.

THE CONSORTIA TWIST

To this point, we have not discussed consortia in any way. For years, universities have been participating in consortia of various types for a number of reasons including resource sharing and access. Consortia at an ever-expanding rate now negotiate and purchase electronic resources for their members. In consortia like OhioLINK,[3] purchase decisions may be recommended to a committee of collection development librarians from across the membership. They are empowered to act for the membership. Such a committee in turn would forward recommendations to the group of directors. The involvement of collection personnel is essential in evaluating and validating the resources that have been recommended and in setting the collection agenda for the consortium. There are some consortia that do more than negotiate and arrange purchase of resources. OhioLINK, for example, not only coordinates the database selection process and negotiates purchase of databases, but also usually mounts the resources on it own servers. This loading of databases on local servers has some specific benefits. The archival responsibility and control of the resource rests with OhioLINK. Such local control allows for stable and reliable web addresses, providing reliable access from either web catalogs or web pages. Of course, as the resources made available through a consortium multiply, they too call for an organizational scheme to facilitate access by users. At minimum, the consortium provides lists of resources. Later resources by type may be required. Lists of particular resources may follow: for example, all the electronic titles purchased by the consortium. Title lists then suggest subdivision into useful subject categories. In these steps, the subject selectors are the appropriate staff to identify and categorize the resource, and are being called upon for this task.

The consortium may also handle linking among all its services. Linking of indexing and abstracting services to related full text can be done centrally by the consortium, usually at the direction or with the advice of subject selectors. This is a nearly self-evident good at the consortia level as it is in member libraries. This is clearly of value to library. On the other hand, how does the user know of those electronic resources at his or her home institution? Is, for example, each of the more than 2500 electronic journals in OhioLINK cataloged and linked from member catalogs? Are they available from the libraries' web pages? Or is there a link to the already created, full OhioLINK list? Once again, these are important questions that need to be decided locally and often with input from subject selectors.

As the process of controlling resources that selectors have chosen has gotten more and more complicated, the manner in which a resource may be accessed may, in fact, help determine whether or not a resource will be selected in the first place. This is not unlike actions taken in the past by selectors who may have preferred to select items for which there was certain indexing rather than others for which clear access would be less certain. Given the cost of many of the electronic resources in question, clear and direct access allows a better chance of getting full use from fiscal investments.

AT WHAT PRICE OR AT NO PRICE

The question of price has always been part of a selector's repertoire of considerations when choosing resources for purchase. This particular consideration looms especially large for many electronic resources. Clearly librarians have always needed to watch the dollars spent and continue to do so. In fact, the cost of many of these resources is a major factor driving the need to provide the widest and clearest access to the titles through the library's database, as well as through web pages of various types. This is fiscal responsibility and a serious professional obligation. New to our experience in the changing environment, however, is the availability of so many high-quality information resources available free-of-charge over the web. Free resources have always been available but getting access to them often required a substantial amount of behind-the-scenes work. Now resources can be made available by the quick creation of a link on a web page. Perhaps it might be accompanied by a brief annotation. So now many free sites can become part of the user's universe with the blessing of the information profession. "Free," in this case, of course, is not exactly free. There needs to be investment of staff time. These resources need to be identified. Then, once again, a number of decisions need to be made and perhaps codified to allow for guidance in the future in this developing area. For example, are the free materials cataloged into the library's database? Is this performed simply at the request of the selector? Or is there a committee charged with setting up an appropriate structure and rules for these resources? How often are these sites reviewed? Does it matter if they are supported through advertisements that appear on the pages? And who determines their appropriateness for which library web pages? Once again, it is subject selectors who possess the appropriate knowledge to make decisions and develop directions.

CONCLUSION

Clearly in the electronic environment, the role of the selector has become more complicated. As electronic resources continue to expand and develop, selectors will continue to be called upon to guide determinations concerning resource organization, access and use, all above and beyond a simple purchase decision. They will be involved in recommending guidelines for selecting sites, for thinking through the user's intellectual progress along chosen web paths on the way to electronic resources. They will be called upon to work with other library colleagues to bring resources as fully and clearly to the user as possible. Clear organization will be a key element in successfully getting the electronic resource to the user or the user to the resource. The process of collection development will have been extended by the need for organization of electronic resources selected.

NOTES

1. Project MUSE is an endeavor launched by Johns Hopkins University Press in collaboration with the Milton S. Eisenhower Library of Johns Hopkins University to provide full text of Johns Hopkins University Press journals to participants through the World Wide Web.

2. JSTOR is a not-for-profit organization conceived through The Andrew W. Mellon Foundation. Its purpose is to convert back issues of paper journals into electronic format allowing for removal of materials from many library shelves while delivering the journals to the desktop. Currently there are over 500 academic institutional participants in the U.S., with more than an additional 100 internationally.

3. OhioLINK is a consortium of college and university libraries in Ohio, along with the State Library of Ohio. It currently serves more than 500,000 students, faculty and staff at 76 institutions, providing access to research databases and full-text resources.

Distance Learning and the Opportunities and Challenges for Libraries

William J. Gibbs

INTRODUCTION

This chapter provides an overview of distance learning and discusses some of the methods and technologies that characterize it. Relevant research about its effectiveness is reported. The chapter explores the challenges faced by libraries attempting to support distance learning and discusses pertinent issues related to collection development. Given recent advances in computer networking technologies coupled with increasing numbers of courses and degree programs delivered entirely on-line, the chapter focuses on the virtual course or online and Web-based distance learning.

DEFINING DISTANCE EDUCATION

Distance learning is a process of teaching, learning, and communicating in which learners and instructors are separated geographically and technology is used to circumvent the instructional gap caused by distance (Willis, 1993; Garrison and Shale, 1990). Distance learning is characterized by the physical separation of students and teacher; a planned instructional course or unit; media forms such as print, mechanical, or electronic to communicate subject matter content; and

[Haworth co-indexing entry note]: "Distance Learning and the Opportunities and Challenges for Libraries." Gibbs, William J. Co-published simultaneously in *Collection Management* (The Haworth Information Press, an imprint of The Haworth Press, Inc.) Vol. 25, No. 1/2, 2000, pp. 115-135; and: *Electronic Collection Management* (ed: Suzan D. McGinnis) The Haworth Information Press, an imprint of The Haworth Press, Inc., 2000, pp. 115-135. Single or multiple copies of this article are available for a fee from The Haworth Document Delivery Service [1-800-342-9678, 9:00 a.m. - 5:00 p.m. (EST). E-mail address: getinfo@haworthpressinc.com].

115

two-way communication (Slade and Kascus, 1996; Heinich, Molenda, Russell, and Smaldino, 1999). In some ways, it affords students greater independence and fosters individualized study. Unlike on-campus programs, adjunct faculty often teach distance courses at localities remote from the home campus (Mathews, 1991); although this trend may be changing as more courses and programs are delivered over the Internet.

Changing demographics and new electronic technologies have engendered innovative approaches of delivering college and university classes to geographically remote students. Compared to all other instructional methods and delivery modes, distance learning is the fastest growing (McIssa and Gunawardena, 1996). In a 1996 survey of 119 members of the Association of Research Libraries, most of the 74 respondents indicated that their institutions were involved in distance learning and one-half of those responding provide instructional support to faculty developing distance courses (Cooper, Dempsey, Menon, and Millson-Martula, 1998). A survey conducted by the U.S. Department of Education in 1995 indicated that one-third of institutions of higher learning offered distance courses and an additional one-quarter of the schools surveyed planned to offer courses in the near future (Hobbs and Bunnell, 1998). This tendency will likely continue as institutions of higher learning employ worldwide computing networks for instructional delivery. As of this writing, educators, educational researchers, and business professionals, among others devote considerable attention and resources to the development of virtual or all-electronic universities in which courses and, in some cases, entire degree programs can be obtained without students traveling to a college or university campus.

MODES OF DISTANCE EDUCATION

For many years, educators offered distance learning in various modalities and delivery formats such as correspondence courses through the postal system (Schrum, 1999). Heinich et al. (1999) discuss several telecommunications technologies used in recent years to deliver distance education courses:

- *Broadcast radio:* radio programs are broadcast from a lecturer to students. As a form of distance learning, broadcast radio is more often used in developing countries and in localities where constraints prohibit other technologies from being employed.

- *Audio teleconference:* in this form of instructional delivery, "a live, two-way conversation using telephone lines or satellites is used to connect people from different localities" (p. 282).
- *Audiographic teleconference:* this type of instructional communications is similar to an audio teleconference but in addition to hearing all class participants, visuals can be sent over the system to be viewed on a television monitor.
- *One-way video, one-way audio:* a televised broadcast in which students do not have an interactive connection to the teacher. Students see and hear the program but can not directly interact with it.
- *One-way video, two-way audio:* a televised broadcast in which students see and hear the teacher. Using a telephone, for example, a two-way communications connection is established to allow students to interact with the teacher.
- *Two-way video, two-way audio:* a televised broadcast that is fully interactive with two-way audio and video communication.

Recent developments in computer networking technologies offer unprecedented opportunities for representing and retrieving information, course interactivity, and collaboration. The Internet and World Wide Web (WWW) broaden the scope of conventional distance education by extending the time and location boundaries in which courses can be delivered (Moore and Lockee, 1999). The virtual classroom, envisioned by the New Jersey Institute of Technology (NJIT), is an instructional environment made possible through computer networking technology. In this environment, all learning activities and instructional communications are through computer software and hardware (Hiltz, 1995a). Students do not travel to on-campus sites or other predetermined off-campus sites. They take part in classes by interacting with a personal computer connected to the Internet. With this Internet connection, learners from unspecified geographic locations can engage in course work that, in some cases, includes real-time interaction through video and audio conferencing. Despite distances, these technologies afford access to individuals and information worldwide allowing today's distance learners to retrieve content, collaborate, and communicate in a highly effective and timely manner (Anderson and Harris, 1997; Hiltz, 1995a).

THE EFFECTIVENESS OF DISTANCE LEARNING

Distance learning is a widely researched topic, particularly the area of instructional television (Roblyer, Edwards, and Havriluk, 1997). In general, learners and instructors react favorably to distance learning and find courses to be useful and appropriate (Schrum, 1999). Several research studies indicate that instruction offered at a distance can be as effective as traditional face-to-face instruction but certain factors must be considered such as:

- Learner background and experience level
- Learner cognitive style
- Diversity of students participating in the course and
- Appropriateness of the content for the learner

Cook and Cook (1991) found that faculty perceived the learning achievement of most (58%) students in off-campus courses to be comparable to that attained by students in on-campus courses. Moreover, faculty thought 31% of off-campus students had increased learning achievement relative to their on-campus counterparts.

Far less research has been done to investigate the effectiveness of the Internet and/or the WWW for instructional delivery. However, Hiltz (1995a) reports that the effectiveness and accessibility of college-level education can be improved through the virtual classroom model or online course delivery and student mastery of course content "is equal or superior to that in the traditional classroom" (p. 243).

A PROFILE OF DISTANCE LEARNERS

Students enrolled in off-campus programs are generally more mature and older than traditional college-age undergraduates; they maintain significant employment and family responsibilities; they are motivated and enthusiastic about course content and off-campus programs; and are committed to their coursework (Pickett and Nielsen, 1991; Silveria and Leonard, 1996; Cook and Cook, 1991). Bush and Damico (1991) state that 65% of students in their off-campus programs are above the age of 25, many of whom are part-time and enrolled in evening courses. The mean age of the distance learner or the returning adult student is in the mid-thirties (Mathews, 1991). Often these students have restricted access to bibliographic information (Angel and Budnick, 1986) and many, because of geographical location, use public instead of academic libraries (Johnson, 1987). They frequently posses inadequate knowledge and experience in library research, electronic informational resources, and technology in general. They expect instructors to be aware of library resources and services and that the library will support them in fulfilling tasks assigned by instructors (Cooper, Dempsey, Menon, and Millson-Martula, 1998).

Schools offering off-campus programs produce individuals equal to their on-campus counterparts (Maggio and Blazek, 1990). In terms of professional achievement, whether students are on-campus or off-campus makes no difference and off-campus students should not be regarded as different (Curren, 1987). Maggio and Blazek (1990) state:

> Both on-campus and off-campus graduates are similar in their undergraduate educational background, membership in state professional association, and participation in continuing education. Neither group does much speech making, or writing of books or articles. Each is equally satisfied with the job; aspirations for positions in the future are similar. Most important, both groups have similar views of the adequacy of their preservice education. (p. 326)

Given distance learner characteristics, particularly their employment and family responsibilities, there is crucial need for instantaneous information support and meeting this need is an important determinant in student success (Silveria and Leonard, 1996). The needs of distance learner are unique and to facilitate user satisfaction, library personnel must attempt to better understand them (Cooper, Dempsey, Menon, and Millson-Martula, 1998).

GUIDELINES FOR DISTANCE LEARNING LIBRARY SERVICES

Issues pertaining to distance learning are becoming increasingly germane to libraries, so much so that in 1998 the Association of College and Research Libraries (ACRL) guidelines for distance learning library services were revised for the following reasons:

Non-traditional study becoming a more commonplace element in higher education; an increase in diversity of educational opportunities; an increase in the number of unique environments where educational opportunities are offered; an increased recognition of the need for library resources and services at locations other than main campuses; an increased concern and demand for equitable services for all students in higher education, no matter where the "classroom" may be; a greater demand for library resources and services by faculty and staff at distance learning sites; and an increase in technological innovations in the transmittal of information and the delivery of courses. To these may be added the decrease in central campus enrollments, the search for most cost-effective sources for post-secondary education, and the appearance and rapid development of the virtual or all-electronic university, having no physical campus of its own. (p. 689)

The potential of distance learning is great and the capacity to provide library services to remote students and instructors presents challenges and opportunities (Aguilar and Kascus, 1991) for libraries not the least of which are defining, developing, maintaining, and providing collections for courses. How to provide collections and information sources are critical issues regardless of whether or not they are provided at off-campus distance sites, local libraries, or by the on-campus library (Silveria and Leonard, 1996). Further, it is clear that distance learners have the same library and information needs as on-campus students do (Dugan, 1997) and a function of library services is to support their needs. The following excerpts taken from the *ACRL Guidelines for Distance Learning Library Services: The Final Version, approved July 1998* offer guidance to libraries for supporting distance programs:

- Access to adequate library services and resources is essential for the attainment of superior academic skills in post-secondary education, regardless of where students, faculty, and programs are located. Members of the distance learning community are entitled to library services and resources equivalent to those provided for students and faculty in traditional campus settings.
- Special funding arrangements, proactive planning, and promotion are necessary to deliver equivalent library services and to maintain quality in distance learning programs. Because students

and faculty in distance learning programs frequently do not have direct access to a full range of library services and materials, equitable distance learning library services are more personalized than might be expected on campus.

* The originating institution is responsible, through its chief administrative officers and governance organizations, for funding and appropriately meeting the information needs of its distance learning programs in support of their teaching, learning, and research. This support should provide ready and equivalent library services and learning resources to all its students, regardless of location.

* The originating institution recognizes the need for services, management, and technical linkages between the library and other complementary resource bases such as computing facilities, instructional media, and telecommunications centers.

* The originating institution is responsible for involving the library administration and other personnel in the detailed analysis of planning, developing, and adding or changing of the distance learning program from the earliest stages onward.

* The library has a primary responsibility of identifying, developing, coordinating, and providing resources and services, which meet both the standard and the unique information needs of the distance learning community.

* Effective and appropriate services for distance learning communities may differ from, but must be equivalent to, those services offered on a traditional campus. (p. 691)

Issues in Collection Development for Distance Learning

In spite of the ACRL's philosophical perspective and guidelines in general, library services to off-campus students are often inadequate. Inadequate funding, changing educational and communication technologies, maintaining educational quality and supporting distance learners and faculty, among other things, frequently impede efforts to support this instructional modality. Providing adequate support to off-campus students requires institutions of higher learning to make "a philosophical as well as economic commitment to providing that support" (Lebowitz, 1997, p. 307).

There are many significant changes occurring in collection development that result from emerging information technology and, at the same time, it faces escalating costs and dwindling financial resources. Individuals with collection development responsibilities are increasingly required to make technically astute decisions about acquisitions and to be knowledgeable of the growing proliferation of electronic media and information delivery tools and means to fund them (Pastine, 1996). They must also understand users' needs and expectations regarding these electronic resources. Given the pervasiveness of electronic resources and variations of formats, it is reasonable that some (see Demas, 1994) propose that cross-functional review boards oversee the integration of new formats and informational specialists, knowledgeable in particular media types such as multimedia or text, be established.

Pastine (1996) states that the collection development librarian today is faced with new problems and issues some of which include, " . . . funding hardware and software related to the new electronic information resources and access; providing new services via the Internet; providing access to full-text online, along with digital images, video and sound; and collecting software and non-bibliographic databases" (p. 11). Personnel must keep pace with emerging technology and corresponding changes in informational formats by maintaining up-to-date technological skills and knowledge. Selectors not only need to understand new electronic resources but also associated hardware and software configurations and standards.

Planning for Distance Learning

In summarizing what the literature reports as the perceived differences between collection development processes for distance learning programs and on-campus programs, Silveria and Leonard (1996) state the following:

1. Procedures developed to provide materials to off-campus users must be more timely and more flexible than those in place for the main campus, in order to better respond to rapidly changing local programs and needs.
2. Standard policies proscribing duplication of books and serials often must be modified or eliminated when dealing with a large

off-campus user population; a certain amount of duplication is advisable when on-campus and off-campus programs are similar, and users are competing for the same resources.
3. Collection development for off-campus users lacks the well-planned systematic approach of main campus collection development; it is more difficult to anticipate future demands and needs than with an established collection and curriculum. (p. 140)

These perceived differences highlight the fact that distance learners and instructors have unique needs and services should be modified to meet them. While it is clear that collection development personnel face challenges, many of which result from technology, several authors emphasize their involvement in the planning of distance programs. Planning is paramount and librarians must be involved in it. As experts in information access and delivery, library personnel are most qualified to advise as to informational needs of faculty and students and to build collections to support these needs. Distance learners frequently do not have access to a reference desk. Their main access to the library is through the Internet and, in some cases, their first use of the collection is the catalog. Despite these facts, schools often lack planning efforts for technology and corresponding collections (Kirk and Bartelstein, 1999). For this reason, librarians must work with distance instructors to provide navigation tools and instruction that permit students to be successful with electronic access (McManus, 1998). Kirk and Bartelstein (1999) provide an example of a course at Johns Hopkins University's Business of Medicine program delivered by two-way videoconference with Internet support. As part of the course planning process, library staff worked with multidisciplinary teams including webmasters and instructional designers to plan the distance program. They served on instructional design planning teams to advise on such matters as library resources, electronic reserve, and copyright law.

Some of the more pioneering planning and cooperative approaches in support of distance learning entail joint ventures with academic and public libraries, computing entities, administrators and faculty in higher education, among others (Kirk and Bartelstein, 1999). When formulating library services for distance learning there are many possibilities but numerous facets including accreditation, guidelines for services, institutional commitment, and the institutional and student environment that need to be well thought-out prior to implementation (Lebowitz, 1997).

Planning: Identify Software Needs

A fundamental process to building collections is assessing needs. In terms of distance learning, assessment must attempt to determine collection needs prior to the beginning of the distance program and modify or update needs once the program is in place. When distance programs are delivered entirely online, user accessibility to collections poses additional considerations for library personnel. In a two-way interactive television course, for example, learners assemble at off-campus sites and typically there is a limited assortment of hardware, which only the instructor operates as learners watch and listen to the lecture. Conversely, in a virtual course, all class participants use computing hardware and software extensively and the configuration of these systems often varies among participants. As a result, collection development personnel must address how the learner receives collection materials, learner technical proficiency, and the capability of students' computing hardware.

The following case example illustrates some of the collection development issues presented by distance learning, specifically online learning. The example demonstrates the role computing software plays in the online environment and the implications for collection developers.

Since 1996, the author offered several distance courses over the Internet. Each course related to educational technology and/or training design and development. Courses were taught completely online without any face-to-face in-class meetings. All class communications and activities were mediated through software. Students enrolled in the classes were not unlike other distance learners. Most were older with work and family responsibilities and enrolled part-time. Their technology skills ranged from computer novice to expert. They were graduate and undergraduate and employed in a variety of occupations including business and industry, health care, military, k-12 education, and higher education. In many cases, they cited the flexibility of taking a course online and an opportunity to learn about the Internet and WWW as reasons for enrolling in an online course.

This discussion focuses on the activities of one course, *Introduction to Educational Technology*. The author has broadly categorized the

instructional activities in which the students and instructor engaged as
(1) organization and delivery of course content; (2) class communica-
tions/collaboration; (3) student delivery of assignments; and (4) evaluation and testing. In each of the four areas, the instructor determined the
format with which to present content and students' capacity to receive
it. He also selected the appropriate software application to support each
instructional activity. It is important to note that software application
needs vary depending on the course and its requirements. Generally, as
the capability (e.g., video and audio conferencing) and interactivity of
the course increases, so will software application needs.

Organization and Delivery of Course Content

The instructor delivered content in a variety of formats including
print and electronic. Students received textbooks, course outline, syllabus, and research articles though the postal system at the beginning
of each semester. The instructor made the course outline and syllabus
available on the WWW and also placed book chapters and research
articles on electronic reserve which students downloaded.

The course presented theoretical principles in the beginning weeks
of the semester which, as time progressed, students applied to real-
world problems using computer software applications. For instance,
topics of study included learning theory and the systematic design of
instruction. Students used these theories and principles to develop a
comprehensive (at least 4 lessons) instructional unit that they presented to the class.

Using the WWW, e-mail, and an electronic mail list, the instructor
delivered weekly lecture notes, assignments, tutorials, and interactive
software samples, among other things. In a typical lesson, students
read Web documents that presented a set of advanced organizers intended to prepare them for the lesson content. Advanced organizers
included the following:

- A short outline of chapter topics.
- A list of learning objectives.
- A list of relevant terminology.
- A lesson summary and a rationale for the topics.

The instructor's lecture notes followed the advanced organizing
documents and largely served to guide students through and rein-

forced outside readings (e.g., textbook, research articles, etc.). The lecture notes also frequently consisted of detailed step-by-step instructions for using a particular software application to accomplish the learning activity. For example, students developed a research report to be presented on the WWW. To accomplish this task, the instructor provided them a set of comprehensive instructions for creating Web documents. Student-to-student and instructor-to-student discussions supplemented each class activity. Much of the class work required group work. Additionally, using the Internet, students interacted with guest lecturers and scholars who possessed expertise in a relevant field of study.

Some of the software applications that the instructor needed to deliver content were Web browser; HTML editor, Portable Document Format (PDF) reader and writer; file transfer software (e.g., WsFTP, Fetch); graphics editor (e.g., Photoshop); email program (e.g., Eudora); word processor (e.g., Microsoft Word); video and audio digitizing and editing software; Macromedia Director; Shockwave; and Microsoft PowerPoint.

Class Communications/Collaboration

In many respects, the success of an online class, like face-to-face classes, depends on the extent to which the students and instructor interact and the quality of their interactions (Hiltz, 1995b). For this reason, the instructor placed a great deal of emphasis on student participation. First, to facilitate class communications and collaboration, the instructor conducted weekly discussion forums. These included Web-based threaded discussion groups as well as discussions through an electronic mail list. Second, students completed several group projects, which necessitated online collaborative work with classmates. Group project discussions and collaborative work were conducted through e-mail, the WWW, electronic mailing list, and online chat. Third, as part of a course requirement, students needed to contribute at least 5 communications each week using e-mail or the mailing list. Other class communications such as questions, comments, and conversations related or unrelated to the course typically took place through the electronic mailing list and e-mail. Some of the software applications needed to support class communications and collaboration included: Web-based discussion forum software; Web-based chatting software; Web browser; HTML editor; PDF reader and writer; file transfer software; and email.

Student Delivery of Assignments and Evaluation and Testing

Students completed assignments that required them to, among other things, conduct research and prepare research papers; create HTML documents; develop a computer-based instructional module; participate in class discussions; complete periodic online quizzes; a comprehensive final examination and a course survey. To complete these requirements students software needs included a Web browser; HTML editor; file transfer software; word processor; graphics editor; Internet connectivity software; email program; and presentation (e.g., Microsoft PowerPoint) and authoring software (e.g., Macromedia Director, Authorware, or HyperStudio). To process the quiz results and feedback, an interactive Web-based quiz program was used. The course survey was Web-based and it was processed using a CGI form processing program.

As illustrated above, computer software is a primary medium through which class communications and instruction take place in the online course and, for this reason software is of paramount importance to instructors and students. Collection development personnel and library personnel, in general, face a host of issues in terms of software support, several of which are presented here. First, it is critical that personnel work with instructors in the course planning to identify software needs and potential problems. Shaughnessy (1995) proposes that personnel should partake in instructional design teams to help libraries provide appropriate and adequate resources. As collections are made available, particularly in electronic format there may be a need to supplement them with instructional materials such as print instructions written for the remote student's perspective, electronic help screens, demonstrations through video or consultation via e-mail, FAX or telephone (Cooper, Dempsey, Menon and Millison-Martula, 1998). Second, the distribution of software applications presents unique problems. Copyright, site licensing, and mode of distribution all must be considered. Since students in the online course do not assemble at off-campus sites, libraries often face a dilemma of how to distribute applications to individuals. For example, the above case example identifies numerous software applications. If a library acquires and then supplies even a few of these applications, distribution and retrieval can be problematic. One plausible approach is to acquire applications that provide a number of integrated tools distributed through the WWW. Several Web-based course development environments provide instructors and students content creation tools, interactive quizzes and surveys, and a host of communications tools. Some programs offer the capability of integrating media (e.g., video, audio) and serve as vehicles to display various file formats such as PowerPoint presentations. The software resides on a server and class participants access it from their desktop with a Web browser. This reduces the number of component applications needed for courses, it provides a common software environment for all users, and it is easily distributed to the individual. WebCT, Web-Course-in-a-Box, CourseInfo are examples of integrated Web-based course development environments that many libraries are purchasing to support courses. Third, it is incumbent for library personnel to establish clearly define roles of software support. As libraries purchase resources for virtual courses, students will invariably need a knowledgeable person with which to trouble-shoot problems and to provide them software assistance and training. If instructors are inadequately trained or are incapable of addressing the technical needs of students, this responsibility may fall on library personnel, which can place inordinate demands on personnel resources.

ADDITIONAL AREAS OF SUPPORT
FOR DISTANCE LEARNING

There is no one model of library service appropriate for all off-campus programs (Fisher, 1991). Lebowitz (1997) suggests that an appropriate mode of service is one that dedicates a unit staffed with a librarian responsible for working with distance learners. This individual would make certain that students obtain all services including user education, reference and referral assistance, and document delivery. Despite the model adopted, services to off-campus students must be comparable to that offered on-campus, which according to Lebowitz (1997) include:

- Instruction in the use of libraries and library resources, either via printed or electronic format, or via telephone;
- Contact information for requesting assistance from the library by telephone, FAX, e-mail, Web site, or snail mail;

- Information about requesting materials not available at local site libraries;
- Quick turnaround time for materials requested from the library collection;
- Quick response to requests for reference assistance and guidance; and
- Quick response to non-library related questions (i.e., who should I ask about . . . ?). (p. 307)

The 1998 ACRL guidelines state that, "The originating institution recognizes the need for service, management, and technical linkages between the library and other complementary resource bases such as computing facilities, instructional media, and telecommunications centers" (p. 691). Hence, library services for distance programs can be multifaceted and include more traditional approaches such as those mentioned above (e.g., reference and circulation), as well as educational technology, media, and computing services, among others. Marchionini and Maurer (1995) point out that libraries share both physical and human resources. Physical resources include such things as books, periodicals, films, software, electronic databases, and projection and computing equipment. It is not uncommon, for instance, for a library's information technology services to supply software and other media for a two-way interactive distance course or provide the computer server where class materials, communications tools, and development software used in a virtual course reside.

Human resources include information and media specialists who provide instructional and research support to teachers, students, and academic programs. The authors refer to this kind of support as "responsive" services. They also refer to "proactive" services in which personnel work with educators to plan instruction or instructional activities and disseminate information to select faculty, students and programs, among other things. Library personnel often work as resources persons responding to student questions and providing research assistance and database expertise. They serve as course developers and instructional designers who plan and create courses and advise instructors on appropriate methods and strategies for using technology to support learning. In these roles, personnel coordinate efforts to design and develop classes, programs, materials, and media for student and instructor use.

At Eastern Illinois University's Booth Library, the department of Media Services helps faculty infuse technology into the educational process by providing both physical and human resources to library users. Physical resources include hardware and software to support research, teaching, and learning. Human resources or personnel provide experiences, support, programs, instructional design consultation, and products aimed to improve faculty and students' technical knowledge and skills and assist them with using technology for teaching and learning. Departmental services are available for both on and off-campus users and are comprised of: (1) instructional technology–faculty and student development; (2) instructional technology project design and development; and (3) faculty development facilities. Each of these areas is discussed below.

Instructional Technology: Faculty and Student Development

This area focuses on improving faculty and student abilities to effectively use emerging technologies for teaching and learning. It serves as a connection between the acquisition of new technologies and their appropriate use. Throughout the academic year, the Library offers demonstrations, courses, and guided hands-on workshops on a variety of topics such as library and electronic resources, the Internet and WWW and associated software, multimedia, the virtual classroom, Web-based virtual course environments, etc. Library personnel conduct many of these sessions in face-to-face classroom settings. While useful for on-campus users, these activities may be inaccessible to people off-campus. Thus, rather than lecture, many library personnel searched for alternative modes of instruction, which were less directive in nature and allowed them to facilitate student learning of research processes and information utilization (Kirk and Bartelstein, 1999). They also considered other means to distribute instruction. This is especially important for online instructors and students because the present state of technology, in many ways, prohibits live lecture.

To support off-campus users, a number of resources are available. In some cases, training is Web-based including online tutorials that correspond with or supplement in-class sessions. Electronic lesson plans, discussion forums, chat rooms, and virtual instructional support and help desks are also available. Kirk and Bartelstein (1999) point out that to support distance learners, libraries are establishing electronic reference services where users can submit questions by e-mail and browse other frequently asked questions online. In this vein, a distance learner or instructor could study a tutorial on searching the ERIC database, creating a PowerPoint presentation, or creating an HTML document and then contact library personnel through email or a Web-discussion forum to pose questions or request additional assistance. Hypertext summaries of on-campus demonstrations (e.g., how to use an electronic database or a Web-based course development tool) and lectures supplemented with video or audio segments can also help to extend services to off-campus users.

Instructional Technology: Project Design and Development

Preparing a course for distance delivery can be a challenging process and often requires more preparation time than a face-to-face course. The development and use of media, mastering hardware and software operations, managing remote students, among other things, can be problematic and time consuming for instructors. When a course is delivered entirely online, these issues are compounded. The virtual course and associated content materials require that students and instructors have expertise with computing hardware and software, networking, multimedia development, and instructional pedagogy. Faculty members are often ill-equipped in these areas or do not have the interest or time to devote to them. In this regard, library personnel work with individual faculty and/or faculty groups who have identified instructional or learning projects in their disciplines. The Project Design and Development area provides instructional design consulting, materials development, programming, graphic design, and photographic services. Personnel in this area design and develop instructionally oriented WWW sites for on and off-campus classes; convert instructional media (e.g., video) from analog to digital format; and program and author instructional applications.

Faculty Development Facilities and Consulting Areas

The physical spaces and facilities used to support distance learning programs often include instructional technology development centers (Pastine, 1996). Coupled with these centers are personnel, hardware, software and other related costs. Media Services strives to provide instructional and developmental facilities for faculty interested in exploring new technologies and ideas. The department created a hands-on workspace available for faculty to use to create computer-based teaching applications and materials. The facility provides hardware, software, media resources, and consulting services.

It is essential that the physical and human resources provided by libraries emerge with technology. Each of the aforementioned service areas requires resource planning and a close working relationship with distance instructors. A thorough knowledge of course requirements is important and from this knowledge software and hardware acquisitions, development efforts, and training can occur. Services to remote users mandates that appropriations be made for individuals unable to use facilities or take part in technology workshops. Alternative modes of training such as online tutorials supported by discussion forums are one of the many ways to offer services to off-campus users.

It is important to note that the capability of distributing distance courses from and to the computer desktop is likely to attract many on-campus faculty members to online learning. As a result, library personnel will have greater opportunity to work with faculty teaching distance courses because they will be located on-campus.

CONCLUSION

This chapter defined distance learning and it various modalities such as two-way interactive television and the virtual course environment. Libraries must address the unique needs of students enrolled in distance courses. Many libraries struggle to provide a level of service comparable to that suggested by the 1998 ACRL guidelines for distance learning library services. Inadequate funding, increasing cost, and insufficient planning, emerging technology, and the skill levels of personnel contribute to the difficulties libraries experience when supporting distance learning. Librarians must update their knowledge and skills to coincide with the rapidly changing technological environment and evolving media formats. This has particular significance for collection development. The growing prevalence of computer technology and other electronic media in library collections requires collection developers to make more technically complex decisions regarding acquisitions. Often they must be aware of system configurations and the standards under which electronic media operate. With the pervasiveness of technology in libraries, collection developers must be technically astute regarding acquisitions. This is especially important in light of the fact that many libraries face dwindling funds and increasing costs.

This chapter also suggested that library services to support distant learning programs are multifaceted covering a broad range of areas such as reference, circulation, collection development, instructional design, educational technology, and media and computing services. Providing instructional design, educational technology, media and computing services frequently presents a conglomeration of potential needs and issues for collection development. A single online course, for example, supported by these areas requires a host of software applications for which collection developers must determine, among other things, their suitability for the collection, technology standards and configuration, copyright releases, and distribution channels to students and faculty.

NOTES

"ACRL Guidelines for Distance Learning Library Services: The Final Version Approved July 1998." *College & Research Libraries News*, October 1998, 689-694.

Anderson, S.E. and Harris, J.B. "Factors associated with amount of use and benefits obtained by users of a statewide educational telecomputing network." *Educational Technology Research and Development*, 45:1, 1997, 19-50.

Aguilar, W. and Kascus, M. "Introduction. In Off-Campus Library Programs In Higher Education." In *Library Trends* (Eds. William Aguilar, Marie Kascus, Lori Keenan), Spring 1991, 39:4, 367-374.

Angel, M.R. and Budnick, C. "Collection development and acquisitions for service to off-campus students." *Library Acquisitions: Practice and Theory*, 10, 1986, 13-24.

Bush, G.L. and Damico, J.A. "Library Services for Remote Campus." In *Off-campus Library Services*, edited by Barton M. Lessin. Metuchen, NJ: Scarecrow, 1991, 6-21.

Cook, J.E. and Cook, M.W. "Faculty Perspectives Regarding Educational Supports in Off-campus Courses." In *Off-campus Library Services*, edited by Barton M. Lessin. Metuchen, NJ: Scarecrow, 1991, 105-115.

Cooper, R., Dempsey, P. R., Menon, V., and Millson-Martula, C. "Remote Library Users—Need and Expectation." *Library Trends*, 47:1, 1998, 1-14.

Curran, C.C. "Dealing With the Distant Learner as Part-time Learner." *Journal of Education for Library and Information Science*, 27:4, 1987, 240-246.

Demas, S. "Collection Development for the Electronic Library: A Conceptual and Organization Model." *Library Hi-Tech*, 12:3, 1994, 71-80.

Dugan, R.E. "Distance Education: Provider and Victim libraries." *The Journal of Academic Librarianship*, July 1997, 315-318.

Fisher, R.K.. "Separate Library Collection for Off-campus Programs: Some Arguments For and Against." In *Off-campus Library Services*, edited by Barton M. Lessin. Metuchen, NJ: Scarecrow, 1991, 149-160.

Garrison, D.R. and Shale, D. (Eds.). *Education at a Distance: From Issues to Practice.* Florida: Krieger Publishing, 1990.

Heinich, R., Molenda, M., Russell, J.D., and Smaldino, S.E. *Instructional Media and Technologies for Learning.* Columbus, Ohio: Merrill, 1999.

Hiltz, R.S. *The Virtual Classroom Learning Without Limits Via Computer Networks.* Norwood, New Jersey: Ablex Publishing Corporation, 1995a.

Hiltz, R.S. "Teaching in a virtual classroom." *In the Proceeding of the International Conference on Computer Assisted Instruction '95*, Taiwan, March 1995b.

Hobbs, J.L. and Bunnell, D.P. "The Emergence of Distance Education and the Challenge to Academic Library Service." *Georgia Library Quarterly*, 35:4, 1998, 6-11.

Johnson, J. "Collection Management for Off-Campus Library Services," *Library Acquisitions: Practice and Theory*, 11:1, 1987, 75-84.

Kirk, E.K., and Bartelstein, A.M. "Libraries Close In On Distance Education. (Librarians Ensure Awareness of Program Shortcomings)." *Library Journal*, 124:6, 1999, 40.

Lebowitz, G. "Library Service to Distant Students: An Equity Issue." *The Journal of Academic Librarianship*, July 1997, 303-308.

Maggio, T.G., and Blazek, R. "On-campus and Off-campus Programs of Accredited Library Schools: A Comparison of Graduates." *Journal of Education for Library and Information Science*, 30:4, 1990, 315-329.

Marchionini, G. and Maurer, H. "The Roles of Digital Libraries in Teaching and Learning." *Communications of the ACM*, April 1995, 38:4, 67-75.

Mathews, A.J. "Accepting the Challenge: Providing Quality Library Services for Distance Education Programs." In *Off-campus Library Services*, edited by Barton M. Lessin. Metuchen, NJ: Scarecrow, 1991, 209-220.

McIssa, M. and Gunawardena, C. "Distance Education." In *Handbook of Research for Educational Communications and Technology*, edited by David Jonassen. New York: Simon & Schuster/Macmillan, 1996, 403-437.

McManus, M.G. "Neither Pandora Nor Cassandra: Library Services and Distance Education in the Next Decade." *College & Research Libraries News*, June 1998, 432-435.

Moore, D.R. and Lockee, B.B. "A Taxonomy of Bandwidth: Consideration and Principles to Guide Practice in the Design and Delivery of Distance Education." In *Educational Media and Technology Yearbook*, edited by Robert Maribe Branch and Mary Ann Fitzgerald. Englewood, Colorado: Libraries Unlimited, Inc. 1999, 64-71.

Pastine, M. "Introduction." In *Collection Development: Pass and Future*, edited by Maureen Pastine. New York: The Haworth Press, Inc., 1996, 1-30.

Pickett, M.J. and Nielsen, B. "Library Development as a Catalyst for Continuing Education Innovation in a Major Research University: A Case Study." In *Off-campus Library Services*, edited by Barton M. Lessin. Metuchen, NJ: Scarecrow, 1991, 188-201.

Roblyer, M.D., Edwards, J. and Havriluk, M.A. *Integrating Educational Technology into Teaching.* Columbus, Ohio: Merrill, 1997.

Schrum, L. "Trends in Distance Learning: Lessons to Inform Practice." In *Educational Media and Technology Yearbook*, edited by Robert Maribe Branch and Mary Ann Fitzgerald. Englewood, Colorado: Libraries Unlimited, Inc., 1999, 11-16.

Shaughnessy, T. Distance learning and libraries. *ARL, Bimonthly Newsletter,* 179 1995, 1-3.

Silveria, J.B and Leonard, B.G. "The Balancing Act: Collection Development in Support of Remote Users in an Extended Campus Setting." In *Collection Development: Past and Future*, edited by Maureen Pastine. New York: The Haworth Press, Inc., 1996, 139-151.

Slade, A.L. and Kascus, M.A. *Library Services for Off-campus and Distance Education: The Second Annotated Bibliography.* Englewood, CO: Libraries Unlimited, 1996.

Willis, B. *Distance Ed. A Practical Guide.* Englewood Cliffs, New Jersey: Educational Technology Publications, 1993.

Some Issues for Collection Developers and Content Managers

Thomas Peters

INTRODUCTION

We need to briefly explore several large issues facing the collection development and content management functions within North American academic libraries as a result of the rapid development of computer networks and digital scholarly and academic information resources. One fascinating outcome of new technological developments is that they often enable us to see old technologies and enduring human projects from fresh perspectives. The emerging techno-economic straitjacket will affect texts, collections, users, the processes of collection development, and the intellectual underpinnings of this sub-discipline of librarianship. Suddenly the old things take on new meanings, new possibilities, and new limitations. The diffusion and maturation of computers and computer networks are doing this to the honored principles and practices of collection development in academic libraries. Computer networks are information systems–the current darling of screen and screen. They are beginning to have profound effects on academic library collections, an older and different type of information system. Computers and computer networks are changing the procedures that gird collection development, the economics of the creation and distribution of scholarly information, what people can and want to do with scholarly texts, and the very nature of the texts them-

[Haworth co-indexing entry note]: "Some Issues for Collection Developers and Content Managers." Peters, Thomas. Co-published simultaneously in *Collection Management* (The Haworth Information Press, an imprint of The Haworth Press, Inc.) Vol. 25, No. 1/2, 2000, pp. 137-153; and: *Electronic Collection Management* (ed: Suzan D. McGinnis) The Haworth Information Press, an imprint of The Haworth Press, Inc., 2000, pp. 137-153. Single or multiple copies of this article are available for a fee from The Haworth Document Delivery Service [1-800-342-9678, 9:00 a.m. - 5:00 p.m. (EST). E-mail address: getinfo@haworthpressinc.com].

137

selves. In short, computers have changed everything–except perhaps the working assumptions and beliefs of the majority of collection development librarians.

Let us scan the current environment for some of the larger issues and implications regarding the relationship between computers (including computer networks) and collection development and content management activities in academic libraries. For several hundred years now two basic units–the monograph and the journal article–have served as the fundamental constructs for a synchronous scholarly communication. The 300-page monograph and the 10-page article have been of tremendous, long lasting benefit to scholarly communication. Because the intent of academic libraries is to foster and facilitate asynchronous scholarly communication (a form of teaching and learning) for a relatively well-defined user population (yet one that almost completely turns over every five years or so), academic libraries have selected, acquired, provided both intellectual and physical access to, and preserved books and journal articles. Within the field of academic librarianship, the sub-discipline known as collection development has been building and assessing these collections.

Although from a user's point of view the book and the journal article are the basic units of study, from the collection developer's standpoint the individual monograph and the journal *title* have been the basic units for selection and management. This situation of simultaneous congruence and incongruence is deeply embedded in the current methods of building print-based academic library collections: both the selector and the user think often in terms of individual monographs (a congruence of attentional granularity), but whereas the user thinks in terms of individual journal articles with highly probable pertinent content, the selector tends to think in terms of journal titles, which over time publish a large number of issues containing articles on a variety of topics (an incongruence of attentional granularity). Throughout the 20th Century, although the portions of the annual materials budgets of academic libraries devoted to monographs and journals have shifted, the basic situation has not changed much. Although there are notable exceptions, in general within academic libraries the established infrastructure for collection development supports a large number of $50 selection decisions, peppered (alas, with increasing frequency) by catastrophic cuts in the number of journal titles currently subscribed to in print format.

The emergence of digital scholarly information in the latter half of the 20th Century does not represent a revolution in this respect, but rather just an acceleration of the fundamental difference between the attentional granularity of the builders of collections and its users. Stated bluntly, the basic units of selection seem to be getting larger, while the basic units of retrieval and use seem to be getting smaller. The economies of scale of building collections seem to be asserting themselves with increasing impatience, while computerized, networked information systems enable users to search for information with amazing precision. Like smart bombs, some search engines now enable searchers to zero in on the best parts of documents (i.e., those parts with the highest frequency of the search terms entered). On the selection side, large databases of journal articles, often containing more than a million individual articles, now can be searched in one fell swoop. Purveyors of online etexts, such as netLibrary, now boast over ten thousand monographs that can be selected either the old-fashioned way (one at a time) or collectively as a ready to search and use online book collection. Although core print and microform collections have been available for acquisition in "one fell swoop" for years, what used to be the atypical way of selecting information has become the typical way of acquiring e-resources. We have gone from painstakingly building collections one brick at a time to some sort of pre-fab collection building. The new era of building online library collections has become very complex very quickly. E-resource selection now also involves various facets (e.g., technical and licensing issues) that typically have not been major concerns to collection management librarians. The guild is justifiably nervous.

THE TECHNO-ECONOMIC STRAITJACKET

In some ways, the emergence of computers and computer systems represent an evolution in information systems, not a revolution. The creation, distribution, and use of scholarly information always have been built as a technological and economic system. This was as true during the high middle ages as it is during the first years of this new millennium. The last half of the 20th Century may have been the economic glory days for the purchase of scholarly information. It was a buyer's market, and buyers had plenty of money to spend. Information technologies were relatively stable, and the combination of a healthy information economy and established technologies resulted in a luxurious sense of collection development as a sort of thought experiment beyond the pale of pressing economic and technological factors. During the last ten to fifteen years, however, the economics of creating, distributing, and using scholarly information have undergone major changes, and we find ourselves having to be much more cognizant of the cost of collection development, including both materials and intellectual labor. We need to explore or develop more efficient ways to identify the texts desired and needed by a population of users, how to acquire those texts, then how to provide intellectual access. Coffman suggests that the traditional approach to collection development hurts users in two ways.[1] First, we waste money purchasing information that the user population may not need, and second, that limits the amount of money available to develop a truly satisfying just-in-time information delivery system. Coffman observes that " . . . the Web and adjacent technologies have begun to offer better and more efficient ways of doing our work for us both on the Web itself and inside our buildings." It will take collection developers a few years to get used to this techno-economic straitjacket.

COSTS AND NOISE

Collection development librarians need to be concerned about two things: the cost of doing business and the amount of noise in the systems of information discovery they are creating. The business of collection development librarians is not building collections, but providing academic information to specific individuals and groups within a defined population of potential users. Noise is superfluous information that distracts the user. Advertising in academic databases often is an example. In general, however, advertisers and purveyors of popular information are working hard to reduce the amount of noise within their systems of information transfer. They want a very high percentage of their messages to be on target, and they aggressively use the new possibilities of online information environments to reduce the noise that clutters broadcast media, such as television and radio. We should not assume that members of an academic community should expect to deal with a more noisy information environment. We need to learn how to reduce the noise in the system, ranging from clunky intellectual access systems such as online catalogs that continue to dutifully record (in

centimeters) how tall a book is to collections that are choked by information of interest to only a very small percentage of users.

MICRO AND META COLLECTIONS

For the majority of the print era, local aggregated collections, such
as those organized and housed in college and university libraries,
made the most sense. Local aggregated collections moved to the forefront because they could outpace nearly all private individual collections in terms of collection strengths, organization, and accessibility.
Locally aggregated collections also made sense because they maxi-
mized access to information for the immediate population. Universities were centers of learning to which teachers and students alike
came, and the library served as a center of information and knowledge.
These localized collections have dominated the modern and early
postmodern eras of humankind, but there was trouble in paradise, and
it wasn't inflation. Although local institutional collections were in the
ascendant during most of the 20th Century, they were based essentially on a medieval model where the centralization of scarce and valuable
information resources was a great value-adding project. Collocation of
information was an obviously good thing. For hundreds of years students and scholars had undertaken secular pilgrimages to these intense
and potentially fruitful centers of information. With the advent of
computer networks in the last quarter of the last century, the access
advantage held by local aggregated collections has diminished. In the
future, micro digital collections (e.g., on personal hard drives) and
meta collections (e.g., consortial or statewide) probably will grab market share from the locally aggregated collections. Main libraries on
college and university campuses probably will not disappear, but their
utility in the overall information universe of the faculty, students, and
staff at these respective institutions will diminish. There will be much
unnecessary wailing and gnashing of teeth over this inevitable development. It is ironic that, while the percentage of the library materials
budget allocated for periodical subscriptions has risen steadily in the
last fifteen years, due in large part to persistent inflation in that sector
of the academic information economy, it is in the area of full-text
journal collections that the value of local collections will deflate soon-
est and most rapidly.

EXPANSION OF GREY LITERATURE

If we do become bound up in a much more stringent techno-economic straitjacket, much scholarly information may be forced out of (or simply drop out of) the for-profit (or at least cost recovery) information economy. Gelfand explores how the nature of the intent, creation, and distribution of grey literature has changed with the advent of computerized information networks and electronic publishing.[2] In the coming decades we could witness a significant increase in the amount and quality of grey literature. Think of all of the PowerPoint presentations upon which scholarly talks have been given, then subsequently made available via the Web. Who is selecting and collecting these interesting scholarly utterances? The stigma of self-publication may lift. Academic collection development librarians will need to take ephemeral literature much more seriously. We probably should begin systematically collecting it on a wide-scale basis with a long-term, institutional commitment to provide intellectual access. As the packaging and distribution of academic information becomes more complex and diverse, academic librarians will need to move away from devoting the lion's share of their time and resources to acquiring printed books and journals.

DISINTEGRATION OF TEXTS

If more scholarly information is created, distributed, accessed, and used online, and if digital rights management (DRM) systems mature to the point where the transfer of payment (whether by the library or the individual) occurs as close to the moment of use as possible, we may witness a steady, perhaps precipitous, disintegration of texts. In a recent discussion paper from the Association of Research Libraries (ARL) Research Collections Committee, Branin, Groen, and Thorin note, "The traditional book and journal as organizing frames for scholarship will likely change as will basic production, distribution, and archiving."[3] The old economics of the production, distribution, and use of academic information objects may not make sense in a computerized, networked information environment. Why should a library or an individual purchase up front the entire published proceedings of a conference when only a few papers are of interest? Journal titles may continue to make sense as indicators of the general editorial quality and subject scope of individual articles, but why should a library or an individual subscribe to an entire journal when individual articles can be found in large databases and purchased singly on demand? Why should a professor ask her students to purchase an entire prepackaged textbook when she will ask them to read only a few of the chapters? The limitations of production and distribution channels based on print-runs and internal combustion engines no longer apply.

VIRTUAL COLLECTIONS

In June 1999 at the School for Scanning in Chicago, a conference sponsored by the Northeast Document Conservation Center (NEDCC), Clifford Lynch from the Coalition for Networked Information (CNI) made a speech in which he mentioned that virtual collections now are possible. The corpus of online non-proprietary, full-text, full-image information has reached sufficient mass to make virtual collection development possible. The collector would construct a virtual space (e.g., a Web site) where full-text information from disparate sources would be virtually collocated and organized into an online collection. If people begin to construct virtual collections, it will be an interesting test of the power of collection management for several reasons. First, it will answer the question concerning the sustainability of the human impulse to collect without any vestige of pride of ownership–neither for the individual nor for an institution. Perhaps it would be better to understand virtual collection development as the logical extension of compiling annotated bibliographies, rather than as a new frontier for collection development proper.

Second, the emergence of virtual collections may be a threat to the dominance of the idea of pan-discipline, Alexandrian collections, either titular or true. Virtual collections will be much more focused topically than the typical real-world academic library collection. Pan-discipline collections have very little value for most potential users of these collections. A pan-discipline collection has value as a totality only to a fairly well defined population–accreditation agencies, the collectors themselves, deans, directors, etc. Pan-discipline collections have value primarily for their extractive qualities. Everyone who uses a pan-discipline collection is trying to extract useful information from it. We were all data miners before data mining was cool. Any miner must answer two basic questions. First, what is the value of that which I hope to extract? If the market value for a precious metal drops, marginal mines often shut down, because the cost-benefit analysis does not pan out. Second, what will it cost me (in terms of either time or money–usually time in library environments) to extract these things of value? For rank and file users of the collection, the immediate task at hand is to mentally (and eventually physically) separate the material potentially of interest from the large mass of material that clearly is not of interest.

Mining data from a print on paper collection in an academic library is a real drag. Digital data may open up a new era for a new type of collection development. We should not assume that alphanumeric data will maintain its current place of prominence. Geography and computer science researchers at the University of California at Santa Barbara are developing the concept of iscapes–information landscapes compiled from dispersed digital resources. Iscapes combine data sets, textual information, and computer models to solve specific problems. The five-year, $5.4 million grant project, officially called the Alexandria Digital Earth Prototype, will rely in part on the Alexandria Digital Library at UC-Santa Barbara, a digital collection of approximately 1.5 terabytes of digital maps, remote-sensing images, and aerial photographs.[4] This type of post-retrieval processing of information is a far cry from simply photocopying ink-on-paper information so that it can be easily transported out of a bricks and mortar academic library edifice. The need and desire to create a personally meaningful information space out of the welter of ambient information has not changed. That human impulse probably existed long before libraries came into existence. Computers and computer networks simply have changed the calculus by which humans satisfy these information needs and cognitive desires.

HOMOGENIZED COLLECTIONS

Some collection developers have wondered if the proliferation of pre-fab digital collections of journal articles and etexts has increased the homogeneity of academic library collections. While we examine the rising degree of homogeneity, we also should ponder the causes and value to the user population of the unique aspects of specific collections. If a collection is strong in nanotechnology, and the user is a nanotechnologist, of course that unique quality of the collection has a high value for that particular user. If, however, two collections contain 100 books on a topic, and if ten percent of the first collection is unique, while 25 percent of the second collection is unique, of what value is the increased uniqueness of a pan-discipline collection to a given user population?

INCREASED USER CONTROL

The techno-economic straitjacket and its potential affects on both collections and texts also will change the social capital of the user population. All of these anticipated developments mean increased control for the actual users of scholarly and academic information. Managing the information discovery space and the objects found in it (and the relationships between the found objects) will become an option for each individual user. Collection development librarians no longer will need to worry about the user interface. The late 20th Century quest for the perfect user interface (which essentially was a utilitarian project–seeking the greatest good for the greatest number of people within the confines of a single user interface) will give way to mass customization. Each individual user, whether wittingly or unwittingly, will design his or her own online information environment. The user interface will become the user's interface. The "my library" projects already underway at several academic libraries (see the hot-linked list of projects at *http://www.library.vcu.edu/mylibrary/ci199.html*) provide a glimpse of future customized interfaces.

PATRON DRIVEN SELECTION

Although it is a truism that it is impossible to have a collection without a collector, the hegemony of bibliographers and subject specialists as the collectors behind the collections may be in danger. Academic librarians in general have not capitalized on and leveraged the knowledge, insights, and feedback of actual patron use of library collections and services. In less than a decade Web site developers have far outpaced us in the ability to exploit actual use to refine and improve future use of their information systems. We have been both profligate and lazy in allowing so many patrons to use these information systems called academic libraries without systematically acquiring and analyzing feedback information from the user population. This does not mean or imply that we must act on every purchase request or suggestion dropped in the suggestion box. It does mean that any designer of any information system should be able to learn much from a deliberate observation of actual use of the information system. In collection management a change in attitude concerning the user's role in the articulation of the information system could have a profound influence on this sub-discipline. Patrons could contribute much to the process of building and refining a collection. Coffman points out that the patron-driven collection development model proposes to use patron selections, suggestions, and behavior as sources of information about what should and should not be added to the local collection.[5] Computer networks certainly make patron-driven models more feasible. For example, patron-driven selection methods are possible in the netLibrary system (www.netlibrary.com). As readers interact with the entire corpus of texts, if one reader elects to examine a full etext, the reader is allowed to do so, but the system notes this first use. When a second reader elects to view the text (or the first reader comes back for a second look), the library automatically acquires the text and adds it to the collection. Unwittingly the readers have selected the text for purchase.

The patron-driven selection model actually simply pushes the collection development function to a higher level, because the question now becomes: Who selects the texts that get added to the corpus of selectable texts, and what criteria are used to select those texts for the larger corpus? Traditional collection development librarians long have feared and suspected that these larger collection development decisions were being made primarily on the basis of economics and distribution agreements, not necessarily on the potential demand for, quality of, and usefulness of the texts themselves.

POST RETRIEVAL PROCESSING

Selectors of e-resources also need to be keenly aware of what users do (or want to do) with e-texts after they have been retrieved. Because reading and photocopying are the two main options with print-based texts, collection developers of traditional print-based collections (ex-

cluding microformats for a moment) did not need to concern themselves much with the possibilities for the post-retrieval processing of
text. Until a few years ago, collection development librarians never
had to worry about what people did with texts after they had retrieved
them. The options for post-retrieval activities were fairly limited. The
texts could circulate, be photocopied, and be read. None of these
processes integrally affected the collection development process.
Computer networks have changed all that. The number of post-retrieval processing options is expanding rapidly, and what people do with
texts after retrieval is now a crucial factor in collection development
decisions. Computer networks have forced collection developers to
think about not only what type of information people want and need
(in terms of subject area and format), but also how they actually use
information. Although the recent crop of computerized dedicated
reading devices, such as the Rocket eBook from Nuvomedia
(www.nuvomedia.com), will survive only if they offer a pleasant reading experience, if they flourish it will be because of the other types of
post-retrieval processing of texts they facilitate. In the future, collection development librarians will need to be knowledgeable of all potential post-retrieval processes.

THE PROCESSES OF COLLECTION DEVELOPMENT
AND MANAGEMENT

The techno-economic straitjacket, along with its possible affects on
collections, texts, and users, also will affect the processes of collection
development. Computer networks have had a great impact on these
processes. Selectors now routinely have access to the OCLC Union
Catalog, online reviews, their own catalogs (perhaps union catalogs as
well), the acquisition system (again, it may be an acquisitions systems
shared by several institutions), publisher Web sites, and usage data
about the use of specific items or subsets of the collection. Selectors
and bibliographers suddenly are confronted with a wealth of management and decision-aiding information that can be delivered to the
desktop in real time just prior to the selection decision. Cognitively
assimilating this wealth of information into a decision system that
must be increasingly efficient and effective is a monumental challenge. As scholars and practitioners of a sub-discipline, collection

development librarians should be keenly interested in how well (or how poorly) they as a group are exploiting this information.

JUST-IN-TIME ACQUISITION

Rather than continue to build collections based on a large number of small just-in-case decisions, we need to continue to explore systems that enable the purchase of information units (either for perpetual ownership or for the right to access for a specified period of time) as close to the moment of use as possible. A pay-per-use information delivery system may not be a fiscal disaster for many libraries. No one wants to return to the days of mediated database searching, where every second online cost money, and the librarian as mediator felt compelled to hold online think time to a minimum. We need to explore acquisition models that delay cash transfers until the moment of need or use, without interfering with the user's goal of virtually unfettered access to information. The development of netLibrary and the current crop of dedicated reading devices open up new possibilities for institutional cash payments as close to the moment of individual use a possible. Collection developers need to pressure the publishers and distributors of scholarly e-resources to explore fair and equitable cash exchange systems. In particular, many publishers seem much more intent on maintaining the current cash flow than on exploring new economic systems for good and broad dissemination of scholarly information. The recent advanced development of distribution systems for commercially viable etexts has resulted in renewed interest in digital rights management (DRM) standards and technologies, so that copyright holders receive some compensation for every use of intellectual property.

TO COLLECT AND PRESERVE

In the good old days of collection development and management, the logically distinguishable human urges to collect and to preserve information were all emotionally and procedurally jumbled together. Selectors often spoke of the information needs of future generations, and they thought about their task as something that had to (and would) stand the test of time. Even many of their micro decisions, such as whether to select the paperbound or hardbound editions of a text, were driven as much by preservation concerns as by the need to meet immediate information needs. The advent of computer networks may have unbundled permanently the need to collect information for the useful half-life of an information object from concerns about the long-term preservation of digital information. Although the issues surrounding the challenge of providing long-term digital archiving for digital information are substantial, now it appears that they can be addressed discretely, without being bound inextricably to issues of how to provide access during the first flush of interest and access.

STOP COLLECTING ALTOGETHER

Perhaps all but the largest academic libraries (e.g., the non-ARL libraries) should simply get out of the collection development business altogether. Adrian Alexander, the executive director of the Big 12 Plus Libraries Consortium (*www.big12plus.org*) and others have suggested that this sub-discipline is moving from the theory and practice of collection management to that of content management in a networked, collaborative, decentralized environment. The danger is that content management could degenerate into commodity trading, with scholarly information traded cheek by jowl with pork bellies. Because the idea of a "local" collection is rooted in the human notion of place, and because the traditional human notion of place seems to have little pertinence in online environments, the value of local collections may be waning. Rather than spend millions (or at least hundreds of thousands) of dollars per year building a collection, perhaps the small and medium-sized academic libraries should focus on meeting the immediate information needs of the defined population in whatever way makes the most sense–that is, the delivery mechanism that is best for the user. This might be purchasing a hardcopy book, but it could be many other things. The focus of this new type of collection management (we would have to think of a new name for this endeavor) would be on connecting the user with potentially pertinent digital information objects as quickly as possible, in a format that is optimal to the user. If a collection of locally owned databases and information objects grew up as a result of the pursuit of this primary focus, it would be a happy, valuable byproduct, but not the main goal. Again, the purpose of collection development ultimately is not to develop collections, but to meet the actual information needs of real members of a defined community of potential users.

A rich scholarly information environment does not need to privilege the text-bearing devices. An environment can be conceived as more than a collection of information objects. In November 1999 the National Academy of Sciences released a report on the future of copyright written by the Committee on Intellectual Property Rights and the Emerging Information Infrastructure. Randall Davis, a professor at MIT and the chair of the committee, was quoted as saying, "But increasing use of licensing also means that information is more an event to be experienced, rather than an artifact to be kept." The prospect of a declining importance for print-based scholarly information could mean that we need to think about information seeking and use more as a sequence of events, an experience, or an interaction with the ambient information environment, rather than as a carefully chosen set of print-based, text-bearing devices.

MIND-FORGED MANACLES

Computers and computer networks have easily and inexorably changed the structure and nature of the distribution system for scholarly and academic information. It is ironic that the print-based latter day Luddites, who refuse to accept the apparently foregone conclusion that the future of most information is digital, often argue or suggest that their print-based dreams of the future have the best interests of future generations of readers in mind. Despite the tremendous impact computers and computer networks have had on collection development and management, scholarly information transfer remains essentially human, from first to last. Computers and computer networks have changed the infrastructure and environment in which this human activity manifests itself. The threat to collection development and collection management is our own mind-forged manacles. What we need to realize is that the distribution system for scholarly information that worked very well in 1965 will, if kept intact with only minor changes, work very poorly in 2005.

PROFESSIONAL SCHISM?

Economics and technology may be pushing collection development and management to transform itself from an art into a science. The traditional manner of engaging in collection development in academic libraries can be summarized thus: hire a librarian with knowledge of both a subject area and of the scholarly publishing industry, give her/him a budget, then let her/him interact with both the local community of users in that subject area and the set of currently available academic publications in that subject area. Repeat as needed with the other major disciplines studied and taught at your college or university. We could call this the traditional method that emphasizes collection development as an art. The method appears to be rooted in the earlier era of substantial departmental, collegiate, and even personal collections, where an individual with significant subject expertise interacting with information about new publications can quickly distinguish the wheat from the chaff. Many traditional print-based academic library collections can be understood as a federation of individually developed, discipline specific collections.

The emergence and maturation of online scholarly information systems has opened up the possibility for a different mode of collection development, based on computerized analysis of collection strengths and weaknesses, publishing trends, and usage information. Usage information often is gathered and reported by the computerized information systems themselves. We could call this new method of collection development a science, based on large-scale data collection and analysis. Of course, the real world of collection development practice is much messier than this, and neither the art nor the science of collection development actually exists in a pure, unalloyed form. Although the economics of these two methods may differ considerably, both methods can result in good collections that meet many of the information needs of a defined community of users. One method is not inherently better than the other. The differences between the two methods, however, are quite pronounced, and over the next few years we may see a widening of a professional schism within the sub-discipline of collection management. The "artists" will wonder what all that number crunching is about, and the "scientists" will wonder how the artists can place such blind faith in the efficacy of their own lights.

CONCLUSION

Readers value any more-than-personal collection of information because it offers ready access to a wide variety of texts that, for whatever combination of reasons, the readers are unwilling or unable to purchase on their own. However the public is defined, any more-than-personal library (pulpy or digital) is a public good. The reading public (including users of academic libraries) reads many more texts than it actually purchases and owns. It seems that this predilection will not change in the near future. Any computer network information distribution system must confront this basic fact. Most of the early text distribution schemes behind the current wave of dedicated reading devices seem to have ignored it. They want to sell all texts at something approaching full retail price to every reader of the texts. They have visions of "super-distribution" systems in mind, where every use of every e-text, no matter how circuitous the route by which the text and the reader found each other, would pay a price for the privilege of reading (and using in other ways) the text. The entire reading public is not ready for such a change, and they will look to libraries to continue to provide both intellectual and eyeball access to a wide variety of needed information. Any distribution model that ignores this seriously risks marginalizing itself and its impact on academic libraries, the collections they contain, and their users. We need to communicate this to the content providers and text aggregators and distributors, then work with them to make the usability, use, and usefulness of digital library collections much richer than what users have experienced with real-world, print-based library collections.

NOTES

1. Coffman, Steve. 1999. Building earth's largest library: Driving into the future. *Searcher* 7(3): 34-37.

2. Gelfand, Julia M. 1999. Grey literature poses new challenges for research libraries. Paper presented at the conference on Creating New Strategies for Cooperative Collection Development, November 12-14, 1999, Aberdeen Woods Conference Center, Atlanta, Georgia, sponsored by the Center for Research Libraries, the Association of Research Libraries, the Council on Library and Information Resources, the International Consortium of Library Consortia, and the Research Libraries Group. Web document located at *http://wwwcrl.uchicago.edu/info/awccconf./awpapersgenl. htm*, last visited on December 10, 1999.

3. Branin, Joseph, Frances Groen, and Suzanne Thorin. 1999. The Changing Nature of Collection Management in Research Libraries: A Discussion Paper. Web document located at *http://www.arl.org/collect/changing.html*, last visited on November 29, 1999.

4. Olsen, Florence. 1999. "Iscapes" combine data sets, computer models, and more to solve problems. *The Chronicle of Higher Education.* Web document located at *http://chronicle.com/free/99/08/99082501t.htm*, last visited on August 26, 1999.

5. Coffman, Steve. 1999b. The response to "building earth's largest library." *Searcher* 7(7): 28-32.

Index

Abstracting, 101-102
Academic libraries
  digital full text periodicals and,
    1-16
  competition and, 8-9
  consortia purchases, 9
  cost-benefit decisions, 7-8
  faculty issues, 9-11
  quality control, 5-7
  staffing issues, 11-13
  student issues, 13
  distance education and, 115-135.
    See also Distance education
  information technology and, 17-36
  accessibility to patrons, 27-29
  communication between
    disciplines, 22-26
  electronic resources coordinator,
    29-25
  reports and statistics, 26-27
  timing of introduction, 19-21
  training and education, 21-22
  interdisciplinary studies and, 51-65
  SPARC and, 37-49
Accessibility, of information
  technology, 27-29
Acquisition costs. *See* Costs; Scholarly
  Publishing and Academic
  Resources Coalition
  (SPARC)
Allen Press, 47
Alternatives Program (SPARC), 45
American Chemical Society (ACS),
  44-45
American Institute of Biological
  Sciences (AIBS), 47
American Institute of Physics (AIP),
  40
American Physical Society (APS), 40
Argus Clearinghouse, 80

Art/science schism, 151
Association for Research Libraries
  (ARL), 37-38. *See also*
  Scholarly Publishing and
  Academic Resources
  Coalition (SPARC)
Association of American Universities
  (AAU), 42-34
Association of American University
  Presses (AAUP), 43
Association of College and Research
  Libraries (ACRL), distance
  learning library services
  guidelines, 119-121,129
Audio teleconferencing, in distance
  education, 117
Augustana College, 1-16

Barschall, Professor Henry, 39-40
Berkeley Public Library, 75
Beyond Bookmarks (Iowa State), 82
Big 12 Chief Academic Officers, 43
Big 12 Plus Libraries Consortium, 47,
  149
BioOne, 47
Bookmarking, 74-75
BUBL Link, 81-82
Budgeting, for interdisciplinary
  studies, 60-61

(University of) California at Santa
  Barbara, 144
California Digital Library
  eScholarship, 46-47
Chapman and Hall publishing
  company, 38-39
CIC-EIC, 87-88
CogNet (MIT), 47